W9-DED-668

MARRIAGE DURING DEPLOYMENT

MARRIAGE DURING DEPLOYMENT

A Memoir of a Military Marriage

Marna Ashburn

ROWMAN & LITTLEFIELD
Lanham • Boulder • New York • London

Published by Rowman & Littlefield
A wholly owned subsidiary of The Rowman & Littlefield Publishing Group,
Inc.
4501 Forbes Boulevard, Suite 200, Lanham, Maryland 20706
www.rowman.com

Unit A, Whitacre Mews, 26-34 Stannary Street, London SE11 4AB

British Library Cataloguing in Publication Information Available

Library of Congress Cataloging-in-Publication Data Available

978-1-4422-6265-2 (cloth : alk. paper)
978-1-4422-6266-9 (electronic)

∞ ™ The paper used in this publication meets the minimum requirements of
American National Standard for Information Sciences Permanence of Paper
for Printed Library Materials, ANSI/NISO Z39.48-1992.

Printed in the United States of America

For my children, with love.

CONTENTS

I

EMOTIONAL EFFECTS OF DEPLOYMENT

The December before Brad left, I often caught him admiring the Christmas decorations in our house. "This is my last holiday here," he said wistfully. "Next year I'll be in Afghanistan."

He gazed with new appreciation at the wreaths hanging in the windows of our cottage home, the blooming red amaryllis on the dining room table, the jars of layered cookie mixes ready to be distributed to teachers and neighbors, and the plaid taffeta stockings with cross-stitched cuffs I'd handmade for the four of us.

"I'm just noticing all the nice touches you do that make a difference," he said. His comments surprised me, coming as they did from a man who ignored me most of the time. His rare compliment, an acknowledgment that how I spent my time and energy—caring for our two children, tending a home, creating the sights, smells, and sounds of daily memories—mattered to him. I wasn't always sure it had.

A few years earlier, we'd purchased a modest house in pretty but pricey southern Rhode Island, where he'd been assigned to an ROTC Department at the local university. Our children, Ellie and Joe, now fifteen and eleven, had settled effortlessly into sports and school activities. I had a wonderful circle of friends, the walkable village life I wanted, an adjunct teaching position at the university, and Naval Station Newport was only thirty minutes away across the bay for health care and the commissary.

Brad had been in the Army for twenty-one years by then since his graduation from West Point in 1985. There'd been challenging and satisfying assignments along the way, but it bothered him that he'd been forced, by bad luck and timing, to sit out the major conflicts, beginning with the rescue of American medical students in Grenada when he was a cadet at the Military Academy. "I'm a CNN commando with four oak leaf clusters," he lamented each time he watched military action unfold on television from the comfort of our living room: Operation Just Cause weeks after he'd been reassigned from the Ranger unit that jumped into Panama, Desert Storm, Haiti, and Operation Iraqi Freedom.

He was an infantry officer and good at what he did, which was planning and operations. Not showing up to the Middle East, he said, wasted his training. "Retiring is like playing for the Red Sox for twenty years and then leaving the year before they win the World Series," he said, repeating the many New Englandisms that had crept into our vernacular in the last four years. He was determined to contribute. It reminded me of what the commercial fishermen in these harsh Atlantic waters said of their chosen profession—"It's not what I do; it's who I am." When Brad spoke of volunteering to deploy for a year, I wasn't surprised.

In early spring, he came home with an announcement. "I got an RFO today. I'm leaving June 3 to Benning, to Afghanistan by June 11. That's coming up fast!" An RFO was a "request for orders" or an administrative cue that reassignment was in the works. Brad was to be an "individual augmentee," a soldier who didn't deploy with a unit but traveled alone to Afghanistan to fill an empty billet.

I could tell he was excited about his upcoming deployment, though he obeyed the old adage, "A good soldier doesn't whistle while he packs his duffel bag." His boss commented to me that Brad seemed more tuned in this year. There was a spring in his step. The wiry retired sergeant major who operated the supply room at the ROTC Department correctly observed that Brad was looking forward to Afghanistan. "I'm going to be relevant again," Brad told me.

The six months prior to his June departure were spent preparing. There were trainings, briefings, uniform issues, health exams and immunizations, security clearances, and reams of paperwork to fill out.

He returned from a medical aid class at the local reserve unit thrilled to show me the latest bandage. "It came from the Israeli army," he said. Injured limbs could be wrapped with just one hand because the bandage had a tension assist. All soldiers were now trained to do IVs. "I found the fifth rib," he announced proudly. Under new doctrine, soldiers didn't just call "Medic!" like in the past. They *were* the medics.

Brad already had the new army combat uniform (ACU) with its greenish-gray, digitalized camouflage pattern that provided cover in both desert and forest. The old woodland battle dress uniform was "so twentieth century" he told me. He held up sand-colored boots. "No more polishing," he declared. "They should have switched to these years ago." I was starting to see that spring in his step.

Years of research and development for the new ACUs resulted in many functional improvements and upgrades. It was made from lighter, quick-drying fabric, unlike its predecessor the battle dress uniform (BDU), which got smelly and heavy like an old canvas tent when it was wet. The top was now roomier and more comfortable, with a zip front rather than buttons that tended to break during frequent washings. The pockets were canted for ergonomic ease and accessibility when the soldier wore body armor and load-bearing equipment. Even the pen and pencil holders were built in near the wrist instead of relying on the ad hoc method of clipping them to buttonholes. In fact, I didn't see any buttonholes on this uniform at all—cuffs and pockets were secured with Velcro closure ("hook-and-loop fastener" as the Army called it) or elastic cord. Gone also was the need to pay the local tailor shop to sew on name tags, rank insignia, and unit patches. All of these now adhered with Velcro, which meant Brad needed only one set to switch among uniforms.

While it improved the mission posture, the new uniform had one serious drawback. "Ouch!" I protested the first time he hugged me. All the scratchy Velcro and razor sharp corners on his chest hit me at eye level. Instead of the expected soft landing, I drew back with lacerations and puncture wounds on my cheek and forehead. It was like embracing a pin cushion. "This will be an occupational hazard at reunions," I muttered.

Brad continued checking off tasks: he took care of his will and power of attorney, closed out his e-mail at work, and reported to the clinic for a round of shots, including another smallpox vaccine, which left a second bulls-eye scar to match the one from childhood. The next day he went to Walmart with a long list of personal, nonissued items he needed to purchase for his deployment.

His bedside reading was all about Afghanistan—*The Kite Runner* and *Bookseller of Kabul*. "Our son would make a good Muslim kid," he said. "He wouldn't have to do any work and he can boss any woman around, even his own mother." We laughed about that, but not too loudly because we didn't want to hurt Joe's feelings. He was our crown prince, the lovable, if unfocused, tow-haired scion of "Sven, the UPS man," Brad had always alleged. How else to explain the Nordic looks and those mythic ice-blue eyes?

When Joe's fifth-grade teacher invited Brad to give a talk to the class, we walked the half mile to the elementary school, he an imposing six-foot figure in his new ACUs and boots. A young girl spied him outside the office and began shouting, "The Army's here! The Army's here!"

Brad spoke to the class for a short time, telling them about his background, where he was going, and what he was going to do there. Afterward, the students peppered him with questions. The girls were curious about relationships and social concerns: "How many places have you lived?" "How will you talk to Joe?" "What will you eat there?" The boys generally stuck to the themes of death and destruction. "What kind of gun do you carry?" "Have you ever blown anything up?" "Is there such a thing as a sniper machine gun?" "Have you ever ridden in a tank?" They had been studying the American Revolution and the Civil War, so they knew about fronts, but Brad told them there were no fronts in this war. "It's a 360-degree battlefield," he said. They looked confused.

We visited with the teacher before we left, and Brad asked her to keep an eye on Joe and let us know if she saw anything that concerned her. "I've already noticed it," she replied. "He talked about his dad leaving, and his eyes teared up." I started crying when I heard that. Up until then, I was under the impression Joe was the resilient military kid, but apparently he was only being stoic to protect us. I reached for the box of tissues every elementary school teacher keeps on his or her desk and dabbed at my eyes, vowing to be more sensitive to Joe.

He was at an enchanting time of life—a boyish eleven-year-old—and he'd been unbelievably affectionate of late. Just that day, he'd hugged me and said "Good morning" as he walked by. The day before, as I read in bed, he brought his own book and climbed up to hang out with me.

I loved and nurtured him, but I wondered, *Who will roughhouse with him this year?* His baseball coach, Bob, and the other dads in our circle were going to have to step up. I would also have to make myself more available to play catch, basketball, and street hockey. When Brad returned home, his son would be twelve, on the cusp of adolescence, and it tore him up to think Joe's childhood would be a memory.

What about Ellie, our preternaturally beautiful, hazel-eyed fifteen-year-old daughter? She was independent, creative, a little high-strung, and very self-possessed. "You've got to use a light touch on this one," my father advised when she was a toddler. Indeed, it seemed she had tugged and strained to set off on an independent course from the beginning. We half joked that she wanted to move into her own place when she was five. In kindergarten, she claimed a corner of the basement play room as her efficiency apartment, making a bed of the toy chest and a breakfast nook of the toddler table and Little Tikes kitchen.

Years of moving as an Army brat had forged her and had been difficult. Her status as the new girl meant repeated iterations of being left out. On the first day of sixth grade at an unfamiliar school, I escorted her to the morning assembly in the gym, where I planned to stay with her and provide moral support because she knew no one. Instead she ordered me to leave, preferring to sit by herself in the bleachers. I choked back tears as I left, one of many times I wondered if we were scarring her permanently with this nomadic military life. But we'd lived in one place—Rhode Island—for four years now, not the three moves in three years we'd done during elementary school. Ellie had completed middle school, which to my mind was the biggest minefield for any growing girl, and was starting her sophomore year at the high school in the fall. With her established friends, track and field in the spring, and Saturday art classes in Providence, she'd designed a happy life for herself.

Despite my husband's pending departure, for the first time in a decade I was optimistic about our union. He'd been so nice to me lately. Before this, his attitude consisted of indifference couched between dismissals; now he was all agreement, attention, and solicitousness. *This* was the man I thought I'd married. Where had he been?

Ours was a marriage designed around being apart. Six months after our wedding, he moved to Fort Benning, Georgia, for an Army school, while I stayed in Savannah to finish my active duty tour. We spent the next half year apart, talking on the telephone (there was no e-mail at the time), sending letters, and seeing each other two weekends a month.

After we added children to the mix, the pattern continued—six months here, ten days there, gone for the summer, six weeks away. I became accustomed to it, but the bond between us suffered.

I wondered how we'd manage our first twelve-month deployment. We'd survived six months to Kosovo and repeated separations during his assignment at the 101st Airborne Division. Still, a year was a long time, and neither one of us was very good on the telephone. I'm a visual person and craved expressions, gestures, and eye contact in communication. Then there was the three- to four-second lag in international calls, which had us stepping on each other in a frustrating, unproductive conversation. E-mail was useful, but it pared down our discourse to pragmatic bullets. Some friends did a video teleconference once during a deployment and warned us against it, so we never used it. "It breaks down your coping mechanisms," they said. We'd have to keep the connection going with calls, e-mails, and old-fashioned letters.

In the months before Brad left, I felt an unease and fragility I hadn't experienced since the terrorist attacks in September 2001. My yoga teacher observed that it was a "tough transition between seasons." (Spring often doesn't come until May in New England.) That explained part of it, but there was something more troubling and insidious about this. I was so jumpy, threadbare, and bedraggled that an overly sentimental commercial for cotton sheets made me cry.

My anxiety was compounded by devastating local news. Three university students, probably drinking, disappeared in a rowboat on the bay one night and drowned. Our little community was grief-stricken. I thought I recognized one of the young men from the photographs in the newspaper, so I checked my old class rosters. Yes, he had been my student in a freshman writing course I'd taught several years earlier. I remembered him well—a counterculture throwback in tie-dyed shirts with an unruly afro, a sweet soul, a musician, and most of his writing had been about being in the wrong place at the wrong time.

The news settled on me like a sodden quilt, compounding my already tender emotional state. Brad's alumni magazine from West Point arrived, and I wept at the pictures of recent graduates who'd been killed in Iraq. The PBS News Hour flashed photographs of our deceased service members, and I cried. When Joe asked me what was wrong, I said, "I'm so sad for their families."

I felt like I was going crazy. "It's anticipatory grief," a friend told me. "I know about it because my mother worked in hospice." My state of mind was a ramped-up version of the anxiety that began on the morning of 9/11 when Brad called from the Balkans to say we were at war. Everything before then took on a halcyon hue. Everything after was blighted with worry, exhaustion, and heartache.

Brad didn't want a farewell. He said it was self-indulgent. "I volunteered for this, remember," he said. But friends told me they wanted a chance to say goodbye. "We'll call it a sendoff, not a party," I told him. I felt strongly about rituals to mark occasions, especially because he was going to a dangerous place and people wanted to wish him the best. Besides—reality check—it would help me if our friends knew he was gone and would reach out to me. We rented the hall at the university Alumni Center, brought in a caterer, invited colleagues and neighbors, and for three hours on a Friday night Brad said goodbye. Though there wasn't a festive air, it was meaningful. "Wait 'til you see the celebration when you get home," a friend said. Because the senator from Rhode Island, Jack Reed, was a veteran who had also graduated from West Point, he made a special point to attend. As part of Military Awareness Day, we raised money for the Fisher House Foundation and our group donated $1,000 to support houses near military medical centers for wounded soldiers and their families.

In the waning weeks before flying out, Brad walked around purposefully claiming the comforts of home, visually preserving in amber freeze frames of the sleeping son, the daughter bent intently over her watercolors, a favorite family dinner of chicken divan. He dashed about, trying to take the children to all their scheduled events—the last time he could deliver them to softball practice, piano, guitar, confirmation class. He didn't want to miss a thing. Even our neighbor across the road said he'd "noticed a shift in the atmosphere over there."

Then it was time for Brad to go. The night before he left he'd spent a long time tucking Ellie and Joe into bed, talking softly and earnestly and unhurriedly with them in closed-door sessions I wasn't allowed to attend. I'm sure there were tears. We'd been down this road before, but each time it delivered fresh emotional blows.

At dawn Brad rose early, abuzz with nervous energy, while I remained cocooned in bed, covers over my head until the very last minute. "Babe, it's time to get up," he finally insisted. We left the children sleeping in their rooms and drove to the airport. A word about airport goodbyes: avoid them like the plague.

We'd had enough of them through the years to know the formula was flawed. There was torturous and prolonged dread as the departure time approached, followed by an awkward public farewell in a transient place with dozens of onlookers. Some military couples drew the line at airport or flight line goodbyes. Instead the soldier said a personal and private goodbye at home and then drove himself to the exit point. The next day, someone gave his wife a lift to pick up the car. This approach was far preferable; however, it wasn't an option this time.

Brad insisted I stay outside the terminal. "I don't want to lose my shit in public," he said. The minivan idled next to the skycap as we embraced one final time, me gingerly shielding my cheek from the Velcro assault. Tears started, then I began crying in the ugliest way possible. All the preparations of the previous months collapsed into this final moment when Brad pushed me away, swung his overstuffed duffel bag onto his broad shoulders, and turned without saying another word. My last image of him was a soldier in gray-green ACUs disappearing into the airport.

Other passengers, perhaps half a dozen of them, had watched us the entire time—the goodbye embrace, the soldier in uniform with a packed duffel bag striding away, and now the despondent wife staring after him and wiping away unapologetic tears. Slack-jawed, they processed the scenario that had just unfolded before them. Eventually I climbed into the empty minivan and drove off into the early morning gray.

2

THE EARLY YEARS

Brad and I met when we were both lieutenants stationed at Hunter Army Airfield, a small garrison in what was then the relatively undiscovered town of Savannah, Georgia. I was an aviation officer flying UH-1 (Huey) helicopters, and he was a platoon leader with the 1st Ranger Battalion. The airfield was on the south side of town, while the historic district was north toward River Street, which was where we junior officers dashed to on Friday and Saturday nights. Downtown offered bars, dancing, and good times for people in our crowd.

One of my good friends was another female lieutenant named Kathy. She was a West Point graduate, smart as a whip, tall, and beautiful, with exotic looks from her Japanese mother. When in Kathy's presence, men tumbled down the evolutionary ladder a few rungs. She commanded all the attention at clubs, while I was her invisible sidekick. "Oh no, please, go dance," I said to her. "I'll sit at the bar and watch our purses." I figured I might get one of her ricochets if I stuck around long enough.

When one of the Army guys started hanging around us, I assumed he was interested in her like all the others were (I knew he was a Ranger by the distinctive high-and-tight haircut). It turned out his tastes ran more to girl-next-door dishwater blondes. He spent all his time talking to me. The next day he called and asked me out to dinner.

Handsome, with striking hazel eyes, he was with one of the line companies in the Ranger Battalion, an elite unit of impossibly sexy, fit young warriors. Because our company orderly rooms were adjacent, I often saw them outfitting equipment and loading trucks. When activity slowed down over there, I knew they had deployed for some real-world training to a country with lots of sand.

Brad and I began dating and quickly became exclusive. I was taken with the easy companionship between us; it seemed like we had known each other a long time. On the weekends when he was in town, we spent afternoons at the downtown Forsyth Park with a picnic, prowled through the shops on River Street, attended concerts, or drove to nearby Hilton Head for the day. We were peers and equals, and there was mutual respect.

About five months after we started dating, he brought up the idea of marriage, purely theoretically. "If we did get married, when would you want to do it?" he asked. This step sounded right to me because I felt so comfortable in the relationship. I had chosen badly in many of my previous romances, comparing them in retrospect to shopping carts with gimpy wheels. Steering them around the grocery store was a struggle from the start, but I stuck with it, hoping for a magical improvement in the next aisle. Then one day I picked a cart with all the ball bearings greased and the wheels aligned and fully functioning. Wow! I glided through the grocery store as if in a dream. I finally understood what a co-worker said about meeting the right one: "You just know."

When we were at my parents' house for Christmas, Brad and I went jogging around the municipal golf course. After the run he said, "Let's go take a look at the river." The next thing I knew, he was on one knee, holding my hand, and presenting me with a beautiful diamond engagement ring. I was shocked and surprised because I hadn't expected this step without a little more discussion, but I happily said "Yes" to his marriage proposal.

We were both twenty-six years old, college-educated professionals, and ready to make a commitment. Six months later, we got married in the Catholic cathedral in downtown Savannah with his father, a deacon, co-presiding. I wasn't Catholic, but it was important to Brad and his family that our vows be a sacrament blessed by a priest. Although my family members were pragmatic Protestants and I never converted to Catholicism, I agreed to a wedding mass.

Later, I would object plenty to the paternalistic Catholic Church, to its invasive turns into our family life, its dogmatic stance on complex matters, its entrenchments in the bone marrow of my husband, and its insidious negative influence on our marriage most of all. It wasn't until after the birth of our first child that I discovered Brad's quivering obeisance to the institution.

Our newlywed phase was enjoyable. We rented a town home not far from the airfield, leaving early for physical training in the morning, working all day, then coming home to have dinner and spend the evenings together, often shooting basketball or bike riding like we always had. There didn't seem to be any adjustment problems in the first few months, except that I slipped right into the sex-stereotyped role of doing all the food shopping, cooking, and cleaning. I was too young and in love to see this as a sign that my status in the relationship had slipped or that the process of erasing me had begun imperceptibly.

Six months after the wedding, Brad was reassigned to Fort Benning, a post about four hours west, to attend a professional course for six months. I still had time left on my assignment in Savannah, so I stayed while he moved out of our place and into a one-bedroom apartment in Columbus, Georgia. From then on we saw each other only on weekends, and not even every weekend depending on his training calendar and my duty schedule. Our marriage began with lots of time apart.

Despite the infrequency of our visits, I got pregnant less than a year after our wedding. By this time, I had already planned to resign my commission and leave active duty once my obligation was completed. While we were both excited to start a family, I would now counsel any young couple to wait at least two years (maybe more) before having a baby. A couple needs that much time to make memories together, get to know one another better, and experience opportunities to develop conflict resolution skills. In light of the half year in different cities, my actual face-to-face time with Brad was limited, and most of it had been spent basking in postnuptial bliss.

Because we were in different cities, he didn't witness me much during my first trimester of pregnancy. "Morning sickness" was misleading—it was all-day nausea. One evening I had to stop the car on the way home from work so I could throw up on the side of the road. At night, I often wouldn't sleep well, so the lethargy the next day was difficult for me, someone who had always been a fitness fanatic.

For the first time I noticed how little tolerance Brad had for my temporary limitations and increased needs. He ignored me if I asked him to pull into a food place when we were driving. He wasn't hungry, so why were we doing this? I had to eat frequent small meals to make it through the day. When we were forced to sleep on the floor of our new apartment because the furniture hadn't arrived yet, he was impatient with my complaints and discomfort. I was five months pregnant.

I prided myself on being low demand and low maintenance and I'd always looked after my own needs, while he unselfconsciously and unhesitatingly looked after his. Now he had to accommodate me more, and the inconvenience bothered him—he wanted a self-sufficient partner. The pregnancy ushered in an era of weight gain and curtailed activity and he didn't like that his hiking, biking, and water skiing buddy was now benched. This woman with her head hanging over the commode bore no resemblance to the vibrant, athletic, and carefree one he'd married.

What I saw more than anything was his disdain for my vulnerability and weakness. Rather than caring for me and cherishing me while I was expecting, he made me feel like a whiner.

After seeing his apathy during the pregnancy, it shouldn't have surprised me when he thought labor was a nonissue. Contractions started and I anticipated a husband who stopped everything and ran around like a crazy man fueled by nerves and excitement, shouting, "I'm gonna be a dad! I'm gonna be a dad!" Instead he went running, announcing as he left, "I don't believe it's labor" (though I was ten days overdue). Even when I threw up the pancake breakfast he made, he remained unconvinced. For the rest of the afternoon, I had a hard time diverting his attention from cleaning the shed or watching the Redskins game on television. "Focus on me!" I wailed. It wounded me that at my most vulnerable moments he was unavailable.

I gave birth to a nine-pound, five-ounce girl after a twelve-hour labor during which I'd had no anesthesia, not even a Tylenol. Later, in what had to be the ultimate hubristic statement, Brad said he "didn't think labor was that hard."

With that absurd comment, we launched our era of parenthood. If he thought I'd expected too much of him when I was pregnant, he had no idea what was coming next.

The long days and sleepless nights of motherhood, along with a touch of postpartum depression, meant I needed emotional support from him that he wasn't prepared to give. He preferred the soft-focus early days of marriage, when weekends spilled with free time for lounging on the beach and I was his good time companion. Now he was faced with a moody, overwrought wife. "I've jumped out of airplanes. I've flown helicopters. Nothing has kicked my butt like being a mother," I said. He thought I was weak.

By the time our daughter was eighteen months old, I was a stay-at-home mom desperately unhappy in her marriage. It wasn't the supportive partnership I'd imagined, and I felt defeated by the Sisyphean demands of household upkeep. To top it off, although I had a beautiful baby girl, I didn't have a job, a salary, a title, or any sense of professional fulfillment. Brad barely acknowledged me, and my morale dropped to an all-time low.

"I see a very lucky woman," Brad responded to my pleas for adjustments in our life. "You don't have to work."

I felt like the proverbial inmate watching the prison gates close on a long and indeterminate sentence. A diffuse sadness crept in as Brad and I became roommates without genuine connection living in the same household.

Because Brad was our economic security, all he had to do was play the breadwinner card and I caved. If anything had to do with Brad's job, whether it was staying late, working weekends, or gobbling up the lion's share of our resources, I accepted it. He brought home the sole paycheck that supported us and I was very protective of him as provider, unwilling to interfere with his excellent professional reputation or anything that could reduce his performance.

I knew the Army was a demanding mistress and he used it to full advantage. When my youngest sister got married on July Fourth weekend, he said he couldn't go because he had to work. It was both a holiday weekend and a family wedding, so leave or a pass could be granted, but he said no, so I went alone.

One afternoon I called him in a panic. The baby wouldn't stop vomiting. She needed to go to the clinic or the emergency room—wherever I could see a doctor. I had been sick in bed with the flu all day and hadn't even changed out of my pajamas. Could he come home early and help me take her to the doctor? It was hard for me to even make this request of him, and I only did it because the baby and I were both ill.

"No," he said. "I have too much paperwork to do at the office."

He had no problem with his sick wife getting dressed and driving the puking baby to the clinic while stopping every five minutes to clean up the mess. In the waiting room, a gentleman kindly fetched a vomit tray for Ellie. As with most military clinics, this one was crowded and it took a long time to be seen by a doctor, who decided after some deliberation with another pediatrician that Ellie wasn't dehydrated and probably didn't need to be admitted to the hospital. Night had fallen by the time I drove home and carried the sleepy, sick baby into the house. Brad was asleep on the couch.

"I didn't know where you were," he said drowsily when I woke him to ask why he didn't come help me at the clinic.

It was one of those times when I was absolutely gobsmacked by my husband's lack of sensitivity and empathy for us, yet I was too tired for an angry confrontation. My head was swimming with fever and congestion, the baby needed medicine and a bottle, and sleep was calling us both. *We will have a conversation about this*, I thought as I slowly climbed the stairs. *Just not today*.

By the time Brad reached the ten-year mark in the Army, he'd survived two RIFs (reductions in force) in the military—one in the late eighties and the second after Operation Desert Storm. Our financial solvency depended on Brad's employment in the Army, and I was determined not to compromise it, especially in light of the touch-and-go climate. Plenty of folks we knew were publicly and unceremoniously drummed out of the service, some with a small severance, others with nothing but a "thanks for coming." It was an era of "what have you done for us lately?" If you didn't get selected for promotion, you had to get out of the Army. If you weren't chosen for a professional school or command, your days were numbered. It was a haunted hayride of gleaming guillotines poised over young officers' heads.

In a small, tight-knit community, everyone knew who the unlucky ones were. They walked furtively around post with out-processing papers as others tactfully averted their eyes. "We should have seen this coming," the shell-shocked wife of one unlucky captain confessed to me. The moving van parked outside their quarters reminded us all what reversals waited in the wings.

It didn't help that we'd cut our teeth in the rough-and-tumble world of an elite unit—the U.S. Army Rangers, where Brad was a lieutenant. They had a history of eating their young. We often nervously joked about the Army's Grim Reaper, the "Black Chinook," a mythic cargo helicopter that appeared when someone screwed up, whether by bad luck, rotten timing, or poor judgment. It could be a DUI, an accidental discharge of a blank round during training, or questionable behavior at the bars on a Saturday night. The offender disappeared in the "Black Chinook" and afterward his name was spoken only in whispers. He was really deposited in another unit outside the Ranger battalion, but the humiliation and rejection were tantamount to career exile.

This was the environment we encountered in an increasingly zero-defect Army. The pink slip lurked around every corner, and it meant no job, no salary, no housing, no health care, and no social support group. That prospect stimulated every childhood fear in me.

For as long as I could remember, my parents lived on the ragged edge financially. We had a big family of five children during the economic recession of the seventies. Dad's pay barely made ends meet and at dinner I could see the strain on his face. The stress eventually split up my parents' marriage, and when they divorced, we children moved with my mom to an apartment on the west side of town, where our struggles began in earnest. Although my mom had some work experience as an administrative assistant, her jobs were low paying. Bill collectors harassed us at all hours (they could do that back then), the bank returned dozens of checks stamped "insufficient funds," and the electricity was turned off for nonpayment several times. One time, folks from church arrived with bags of donated groceries for us.

As an adult I was terrified of lack, especially with a baby at home whom I dearly wanted to care for myself. Brad provided financial security as long as he was considered a good soldier. Rather than make demands on him that might distract his focus, I remained silent even at the expense of my own happiness and well-being. With no paycheck to contribute, I had surrendered all economic power in the marriage, which, as it turned out, was the only power there was.

Brad's frequent absences as an active duty soldier had enabled us to stay married for so long. In fact, they were probably the key to its longevity—seventeen years by the time of the Afghanistan deployment. The state of our marriage, however, was a source of sadness to us both. In family matters, we were co-administrators and serviceable parents, but not loving partners. If the seasons of a marriage could be circumscribed by metaphor, we weren't in the flush of spring or summer's fullness, but in an autumn frost with a thin film of ice covering our couplehood. We were living together but not making a life together.

In our marital détente, we didn't argue and bicker, but we didn't interact much either. It was peaceful indifference. We were spectral presences in one another's lives. Since the birth of our first baby, we had set off on divergent paths, becoming increasingly off course as husband and wife. I felt loss and disappointment over this—he did too—but we weren't sure what to do about it. Four marriage counselors had helped stanch the bleeding at crisis points along the way, enough for us to carry on at least. The therapists contributed insights—there were "clouds of resentment" between us, one said. "Marna needs more emotional support," said another.

None of them had gotten to the heart of the matter, but even I didn't know what it was. I circled the shadowy mass, looking for an angle that would crack the code. I poured my soul out in journals and confided with close friends, but never arrived at a satisfying understanding. It remained a complicated calculus problem that I couldn't solve.

One morning not long after Brad departed to Afghanistan, I was in bed when I heard huge earth movers rumble past the house. They turned into the driveway at the far end of our cul-de-sac, home to high school sweethearts who were now parents of two young boys. Ray was a swarthy commercial fisherman who drove the biggest black pickup truck I'd ever seen; his brunette, chain-smoking wife, Sandy, had stopped working as a dietary aide in the hospital after their first child was born. Sandy and Ray were a little rough around the edges but they were decent, salt-of-the-earth types.

The first buyers in this subdivision, they'd already built an addition on to their salt box. She bragged that they now had the priciest home in the neighborhood, an assessment based purely on square footage because their dwelling looked like an awkward Legos creation. The single-story great room they'd spliced to the backside had enough space for a Foosball table, several Barcaloungers and pub-back couches, an aquarium, and a seventy-inch high-definition television mounted on the wall.

But they weren't finished. Along with the mock, small-scale fishing boat and deluxe playground for the boys in the backyard, they planned to level and clear the wooded lot behind their house (which they'd purchased) for an expanse large enough to put a trampoline, a de facto ball field, and a two-thousand-square-foot garage in which to store their fishing gear.

Which was what they were starting that fine morning in June when I heard the heavy machinery.

Next door to them lived Mr. and Mrs. Hippy, a fortyish couple who couldn't be more different from Mr. and Mrs. Big Truck. Liberal and cerebral, they did grant-funded work at an Ivy League college. They looked creepily like brother and sister, both blondes, he with a groomed goatee and erudite glasses, she usually makeupless with straight long hair. He cut the grass with a rotary push mower, she cooked vegetarian, and they didn't own a television. Their politics were upright and sanctimonious. Right before Brad deployed, they attended a rally to, as Mrs. Hippy told me, "get the president to listen to the American people and get out of Iraq."

They lived for their two young sons. I often saw them set off *en famille* for a walk (sometimes three a day, rain or shine)—tow-headed toddlers in matching Brown University sweatshirts pushed in a double stroller, with the cat following a respectful distance behind.

Mr. and Mrs. Hippy bought the house at the dead end because it was tucked away and private. The backyard was surrounded by trees and undergrowth, providing a shaded haven for their young family. In theory, they liked to neighbor, but they wanted to do it strictly on their own terms, so one of the first things they did was install a fence around their entire property with a gated driveway barricading everyone out. Then they complained that our neighborhood didn't socialize.

I could take them in small doses, but Mrs. Hippy's self-absorption and incessant talking exhausted me. I don't think I ever finished a sentence in her presence. Our discourse went something like this: I began by saying, "I had an architect over to give me some ideas on—" and she interrupted, "We were going to build a garage but it cost too much. We wanted a detached garage next to the house with a covered walkway to the back yard. Do you know what that is? I don't know what it's called."

"A dog trot," I said.

"Oh! You're building one too?" she asked.

"No," I answered, and left it at that. She didn't notice my non-answer. It wasn't a sincere question anyway, just a badly disguised segue into her favorite subjects—her house, her garden, their lives in Portland, Oregon, or the brilliant giftedness of their boys. With Mrs. Hippy, I prepped myself not to expect satisfying, well-explored conversations, but dead-end monologues (hers).

I'm naturally reserved and a good listener, so I did this when Mrs. Hippy came over to vent about what happened with the earth movers. Mr. Big Truck had hired them to rip out the tree line dividing their yards. Mrs. Hippy freaked out at the noise and danger. She'd had no warning of this; it came as a huge surprise. She needed to get her two boys to safety and the rabbit hutch to the opposite side of the yard. It was all so *scary*. She begged Mr. Big Truck to stop and give her a chance to save her family. Did he forget they wanted *privacy*? They *needed the shade*. What was he doing? Those were *trees*, for God's sake.

Mr. Big Truck wasn't the kind of person who took kindly to people telling him what he could and could not do on his own property. Accounts of his actual response varied, but Mrs. Hippy said he yelled at her. Mr. Big Truck said he merely shouted at the workers to follow instructions and "tear it all out."

Trembling, Mrs. Hippy corralled her toddlers into the house and called her husband at work. There were men next door with construction equipment, she said. Mr. Big Truck was screaming at her. It was frightening. She felt threatened.

This I knew for sure because it was recounted to me word for word by all parties: Mr. Hippy called Mr. Big Truck at home and said, "I don't know what's going on there but quit yelling at my wife."

"I wasn't yelling at her," Mr. Big Truck said.

"She said you were and I want you to stop," Mr. Hippy insisted.

As Mrs. Hippy recited her lengthy tale of woe, I nodded mutely, not wishing to get involved, but when I heard those words "stop yelling at my wife," it felt like my solar plexus had been slammed by a two by four.

This problem in my marriage I'd circled for years, unwilling or unable to articulate, revealed itself to me in this unlikely exchange. Missing from my life was a partner who, with no questions asked, would show up with guns blazing to defend me. He had my back. I could always depend on him.

Instead, throughout the marriage, Brad's first instinct was to dismiss me. He offered the benefit of the doubt not to me—his wife—but to the other party. He would have asked, "What did you say to make Mr. Big Truck yell at you?" or "Quit freaking out. I'll go over and apologize when I get home."

No wonder I couldn't come to grips with the issue—it was too painful. I felt invisible to the primary person in my life. Not only was he not in my corner, he didn't even have me in his field of vision.

Brad provided for me but didn't protect me. That essential us-against-the-world understanding, the notion that "arm in arm we'll face what comes," had been missing in my marriage. I had always believed it was a given, especially in a military marriage in which we frequently found ourselves dropped in unfamiliar territory among strangers, a continent away from the nearest relative, staring at each other in some God-forsaken government quarters while we ate cold pizza and slept on borrowed air mattresses until the household goods arrived. What other promise could I cling to except that we'd grip hands and get through this together? At least that's what I always thought.

My myth was so insistent that for years I ignored the glaring disparity between my narrative and reality. To paraphrase Elizabeth Gilbert in *Eat, Pray, Love*, I projected upon Brad all sorts of good qualities that he had never actually cultivated in himself.

Once the duct tape was ripped from my eyes, all the early disappointments and letdowns in the marriage came flooding into my consciousness, almost knocking me out with their emotional impact. The sense of abandonment I experienced when I was in labor with our first child and Brad left to go jogging; the refusal to come home when the baby and I were both sick and needed him. More recently, he proceeded with plans for a promotion party, although the date conflicted with my comprehensive examination for the Master's degree I'd been pursuing for three years.

I was coming to grips with the disappointment I'd long felt in a vague way but had instead averted my eyes and rationalized behaviors. I accepted the falsehood that Brad and I were supporting one another in the golden circle of our vows because it gave me the sense of security I so desperately wanted, but it turned out to be a false sense. Mr. and Mrs. Hippy had inadvertently switched on the mercury vapor lights, illuminating misgivings I'd kept shrouded in darkness for so long.

From the start my marriage had involved long periods apart, and I was lonely when Brad was gone. I just realized I was lonely when he was home too.

3

MANAGING THE RHYTHMS AND DEMANDS OF DAILY LIFE

I reacted to Brad's departure with a mixture of anxiety and relief. While he wouldn't be leading patrols in Taliban strongholds or escorting supply convoys through enemy territory—he was to oversee the development of an Afghan military academy similar to West Point—there were dangers lurking everywhere for American service members in the Middle East. The scourge of improvised explosive devices (IEDs) was especially frightening.

I was also nervous about handling everything on the home front by myself. In the past, I'd managed a six-month deployment while Brad went to Kosovo, but whether I could have lasted another six months was debatable. Both children were in grade school then, and I was working on my Master's degree while teaching college composition, so there were considerable demands besides solo parenting. Brad's absence back then coincided with the terrorist attacks of 9/11, and an e-mail from the command group at the 101st Airborne Division (where he was assigned) warned us that his battalion would return to Fort Campbell long enough to refit, reorganize, and then deploy to the Middle East *for years*.

How will I manage, I wondered at the time, when I'm reduced to fumes after four months?

In the end, he came home from Kosovo as scheduled and didn't redeploy until four years later, volunteering for it this time. A neighbor at Fort Campbell explained it this way: "Better for us to take care of this now so our kids won't have to do it later."

Spring had been pockmarked with Brad's preparations for Afghanistan, and I was ready for the protracted leave-taking to end. There had been farewells with the ROTC Department, a sendoff, relatives visiting, friends stopping by, folks wanting to get together one last time, and an invitation to toss out the first pitch at the university baseball game. With no schedule and nothing fixed like a predictable workday, life was running in fits and starts. As soon as I could reassure myself with "daili-ness"—regular meal times and bed times and each child's appointed activities penned in the blotter—I could convince myself I was capable of handling twelve months of it myself. The job was easier once we established a routine.

Because here was the dirty little secret harbored by military spouses since time immemorial: predictability was more important than presence. Twelve contiguous months blocked out on the calendar as "Deployment" were immutable, nonnegotiable, and therefore accommodated as a fact of life, like gravity or magnetic north. Contrast that with the Whac-a-Mole game at high op-tempo divisions like Fort Bragg or Fort Campbell, where the troops darted in and out like eels at unpredictable intervals—a month and a half, two weeks, ten days—upending plans and contributing to a state of perpetual imbalance.

Brad's constant presence the last several weeks had created its own unique brand of chaos. It felt like I was trapped in a pinball machine, constantly ricocheting and reacting to his "contributions." Existing in a communication blackout, he undertook tasks without mentioning them to me, like reinstalling all the screens on the windows. "Did you wash them off first?" I asked when I got home. "No." I pointed out the spider webs, dust, and dried bug carcasses in the corners. "They all needed a good hosing down." Brad just shrugged and moved on.

His compulsion to throw things away as he straightened up was a problem. One day he caught me on my hands and knees on the kitchen counter with my head buried deep in the spice cabinet. "I know I have a jar of capers in here somewhere," I insisted. "Oh, I tossed those," he said nonchalantly. "We never used them." He didn't see me rolling my eyes because my face was wedged somewhere between allspice and dill. Who shopped for the food? Who did the cooking? Who ran the kitchen? Me, that's who. He had no business purging my provisions.

Another time I tore apart the basement looking for an empty box and some bubble wrap I'd kept for shipping packages. "Do you know where it is?" I asked Brad. "I need to mail something."

"I recycled those last week," he said. My seemingly simple task now involved going to the store to purchase a box and packing supplies, then returning to the house to prepare the mailing, and then going out again to the post office. There went my morning. How cavalierly he created extra work for me.

During his energetic clean-up efforts, he often swept a stack of un-paid bills or a borrowed item from the kitchen counter to the top shelf at the back of the upstairs closet. Or instead of storing the ropes in the boat where they were usually kept, he stashed them in a place known only to him under the wheelbarrow behind the bicycles, delaying my outing because I couldn't load the kayak. I found he'd swiped the last twenty dollars from my wallet when I tried to pay at the Burger King drive thru. Or what of my favorite royal blue cashmere sweater pur-chased at Harrod's in London, which he washed, then threw into the dryer and shrank to baby doll proportions in a commendable but care-less attempt at laundry?

The onslaught was particularly bad during his flurry of preparations. "Brad, where is the lawn mower??" I e-mailed him urgently once he was in Afghanistan. "I gave it away," he said. "You told me you wanted to hire a lawn service." I never said anything about getting rid of the lawn mower though.

Unfortunately, I couldn't get him to understand the concept of men-tioning things to me as, or better yet before, he did them ("Hey, I thought I'd wash this sweater"). I didn't want him to ask permission, just make me aware of the situation. Home, family, and children were my wheelhouse. He was only trying to be helpful, but without proper communication, he undermined me. After a particularly frustrating in-cident (I found out he had let an insurance policy on me lapse without mentioning it), I ranted about his habit of working in a vacuum.

"I don't go to your office and reorganize your files when you're not there. I run this house. I. Need. To. Know," I screamed. I may have also slammed my fist on the table to emphasize each word.

A family member once said of her husband, who traveled a lot as a defense contractor, "Things just run better when he is gone." Another exasperated Navy wife said her husband "needs to go out to sea. He's just in the way." It was harsh, but I understood.

Brad knew enough to be a nuisance, but not enough to be helpful. Consequently, he put me in a twitchy state of vigilance, trying to anticipate his next move. And (this won't surprise anyone who is married to a military guy) he didn't like to take instruction, suggestions, or guidance from me.

That's why his removal felt a little like relief. I had dominion over my house once again. This was a sad fact of military marriages: they were unions designed around being apart, and they functioned more efficiently that way. As a couple, we'd probably spent more time in different zip codes than the same one. His absence was normal, his presence disruptive. Brad was a stranger in a strange land here.

The weeks following Brad's departure were ones of transition and adjustment. The abrupt end to the adrenaline-fueled pre-deployment tempo was quickly replaced with the no-doubt-about-it reality of twelve long months ahead of me. It was like the circus train chugged out of town and left the piles of confetti for me to sweep up. I wasn't exactly drowning in sorrow, but certainly treading in it for quite some time. The stress of it all made me want to burst into tears for no other reason than we were out of butter.

At home I was confronted with upkeep that had been neglected during the hectic lead up to his departure. My house was a wreck; there was plowable dust and clutter on every surface. Here a stack of receipts to file. There a basket of t-shirts to fold. Here an overflowing recycle bin. There a ream of insurance paperwork. Here team patches to sew on a baseball jersey. There a clogged drain.

"Overwhelmed" described it. I had to cook every meal, do all the driving, attend end-of-year school functions, and complete endless tasks associated with running a household. The urgency of constant demands wore me out.

One night not long after Brad left, an electrical storm knocked out both alarm clocks. I woke up at five minutes after seven, not my usual six a.m., and rushed downstairs to rouse Ellie, who had to be at school by 7:30. Then I gave a shout to Joe to get going. Both kids walked into the kitchen where I was toasting bagels and told me simultaneously they had special assignments that morning. "I have to get to school early and study for a Spanish quiz," Ellie announced. Joe said, "I forgot I'm supposed to write a paragraph about a public health issue." I shoved the bagel and orange juice in front of him and rummaged through the recycle bin. "Here," I slapped a *Providence Journal* down on the counter. "A case of tuberculosis has been reported. That's a public health issue. Read this while you eat."

Glancing toward Ellie, who had asked me if I could French braid her hair, I shook my head. "Not today. Finish getting ready while I pack your lunch." I hustled her out the door to the waiting minivan, reminding Joe over my shoulder to brush his teeth before he left. Our neighbor, mother of the twins Max and Ted (Joe's best friends), gave him a ride every morning, but he had to get over to their house.

"Mom!" he yelled back. "What's tuberculosis?"

"Google it!" I said, as I fled the house in yoga pants and flip flops, still sporting bed head and morning breath. At least I wasn't still wearing my pajamas and robe.

Later, with the hectic routine finished and both children in school, I sat at the breakfast bar hunched over a cup of coffee. It was not quite nine and my head was spinning. The kitchen counters were covered with the detritus of the morning; the dishwasher was still full of clean dishes and both sinks overflowed with dirty ones. Because the refrigerator and pantry were practically empty, my first priority after I showered was to shop at the commissary. The Navy base was thirty minutes away, so that was a three-hour round trip.

A knock at the kitchen door interrupted my frantic plotting. Sara, the women I'd hired to clean my house twice a month, stood there in her sinewy runner's body glory, overbleached hair pulled back into a girlish ponytail that emphasized her high cheek bones and tanning booth color. But this wasn't her week. What was she doing here?

"Did you need me today?" she asked. "I couldn't remember."

"Yes, yes, I need you today!" I practically hugged her. "I want you to come every week," I impulsively said. "I can't do this by myself."

So began our arrangement, one of the best decisions I made while Brad was deployed. Sara came for three hours every Thursday and did the basics: bathrooms, kitchen, floors, vacuuming, dusting, trash. Admittedly, these were tasks my children and I could have done—plenty of people do them without help—but the time before Sara started was a disaster. My days were spent spinning from untidy hallways to disheveled rooms. Everywhere I looked there was a mess, and I couldn't cross the threshold in my home without feeling anxiety.

The notion of a paid housekeeper originally offended my Midwestern thriftiness and self-sufficiency, but I got over it. Between double parent duties, I had plenty on my plate. So I ignored my inner "do it yourselfer" and arranged for help, financed with Brad's hazardous duty pay. It seemed an appropriate use for the extra income and turned out to be money well spent. Sure, we could have stashed the equivalent amount of cash in an IRA or vacation fund, but with my shot nerves and exhaustion, would I even last twelve months to enjoy it?

Don't get me wrong—I didn't give up housework entirely, reach for my bon-bons, and lounge in front of soap operas all day. Other responsibilities still faced me, more like a hill than a mountain now that Sara had taken over the routine ones. While she busied herself mopping the kitchen floor and emptying trash cans, I tended to the tasks only I, the household manager, could do. I balanced the checkbook, paid bills, planned meals, reorganized the pantry, shopped for food, dropped off recycling and dry cleaning, washed and folded laundry, mended clothes, made minor home repairs, scheduled doctors' appointments, and completed other administrivia. Between our concerted efforts each Thursday, the home lurched along in a satisfying, if uneven, rhythm.

On days I wasn't there, Sara let herself in with a spare key. Then later, when I opened my front door, a gorgeous, peaceful *aaahhh* moment awaited me. Polished surfaces gleamed, citrus smells wafted about, and the rooms radiated order and neatness. I felt as magical as Mary Poppins, able to straighten the nursery with a snap of her fingers.

It was a small measure of mastery, but I savored it. The change in my attitude was remarkable—such a difference from when I arrived home, caught a glimpse of the disarray, and sank into a defeated mood.

In return for the added expense of Sara, I was a happier, more patient, and engaged mother and wife. The principle could easily be applied to any extra maintenance costs during deployment, whether it was yard work help or eating out more than usual. I had to override a conflicted inner voice, but for our family, Sara's fee was worth it.

As my neighbor, Mrs. Hippy, counseled, "Let go of things that it makes sense and feels good to let go of." There was love work and there was leg work and I was learning I didn't have to do everything.

Joe and I removed the row of cheap aluminum hooks from the tongue-in-groove paneling on the mudroom wall. It was tough going at first until we realized Joe had the drill rotating in the wrong direction. Once we fixed that, things got much easier. I reached for the package containing the large brass hat hooks we were installing. "Wouldn't it be funny if we screwed these hooks in upside down?" I said, trying to cajole Joe into a better mood. He clearly didn't want to be helping with this project. He wanted to skateboard! Or go see the twins!

"What's the definition of child abuse in Rhode Island?" he muttered under his breath. I shook with laughter because the idea of him being mistreated bordered on the absurd. My housekeeper did most of the grunt work around the house, and he didn't even keep his room neat. Because it was his private sanctum of squalor, I just closed the door.

"I mean it Mom," he protested earnestly. "You name one kid who has to make dinner twice a week *and* do dishes twice a week. Just name one kid we know. None of them!"

He was referring to our new household system. At first I posted a cheerful sign in the kitchen with the headline "Thanks for Doing Your Part" in lovely italic script. I didn't want to sound negative and dictatorial, but to model that we all had to pitch in.

"Mom, it's a chore chart," Joe lectured. "Just call it what it is."

I took down the soft-sell version and replaced it with Chore Chart 2.0. It was still Pinterest-fun with seven Post-It notes—one for each day of the week—in bright pinks, oranges, and limes. The jobs for the day, including mine, were listed on the notes. Each person prepared supper twice a week, and on two other days he or she was responsible for keeping the kitchen neat, including emptying the dishwasher, cleaning up after meals, and washing pans.

I figured if we did the basic load of tasks, we would stay on top of things. Each child also had to write their Dad an e-mail once a week and practice guitar every day.

As for me, I had the minimum stuff laid out. I scheduled when to make grocery lists, go food shopping, water plants, pay bills, do laundry, and balance the checkbook. These seemingly trivial tasks kept the household from descending into entropy.

Every evening we had a mandatory "Ten-Minute Tidy" (another too-cute title for which I had scorn heaped upon me by my children). We turned the music up loud, set the timer, and charged around the house picking up items and putting them away.

I promised them daily allowance payable on Friday for completing their chores without being reminded. "That's not fair," Joe complained bitterly, but he complied for the most part. On the day he neglected his kitchen cleanup, he got up early the next morning and did it before breakfast. I offered him absolution—and cold, hard cash.

This system kept me from constantly badgering Ellie and Joe. I didn't want to be the heavy all the time, constantly fussing at them to do this or that whenever they were home, especially with no other parent to shoulder the burden occasionally. They would just learn to associate me with browbeating. Under this plan, the visual reminders were right by the mud room, where they could be seen several times a day.

On Fridays there was no organized dinner. We had a "get-your-own" night in which everyone foraged for leftovers. Sometimes I just opened a cup of yogurt, Ellie made a salad, and Joe chowed down on leftover pizza in front of the television. This casual break in routine proved so popular that Ellie or Joe often asked "Can we have a get-your-own night?"

On the other nights, we ate dinner together. Each person prepared the meal twice a week. Joe and Ellie told me what they wanted to make and I purchased the food at the commissary. Ellie, a fine cook and avowed vegetarian since middle school, was partial to savory soups and dishes containing eggplant. Her homemade cream of tomato soup, hunks of peasant bread on the side, was sublime. I'd only had the insipid version from a can, and she made me see what I'd been missing.

At age eleven, Joe had an offbeat approach to cooking, but he got the job done. His early menus included frozen buffalo chicken wings re-heated in the oven and salad poured out of a bag. Not wanting to discourage him, we always greeted his efforts with an overabundance of praise and positive reinforcement. He soon learned to make a mean blue plate special of grilled cheese and potato chips. On other days he fried burgers or created mile-high deli sandwiches ("Dagwoods," we called them).

Over time his indentured servitude evolved into more confident and sophisticated culinary expression. My visiting sister once observed him wander into the kitchen at lunch time, pull out an armload of ingre-dients from the refrigerator, and make himself a wrap of sliced chicken, tomatoes, pesto mayonnaise, and shaved Parmesan cheese. "Most kids just eat a sleeve of saltines," she said.

As Joe discovered his inner chef, his meals got fancier, like sautéed shrimp atop a salad of spinach, baby carrots, bleu cheese, and sliced cucumbers from our garden. Yet some obnoxious behavior also emerged, making me wonder if I'd created a monster. "This isn't made with homemade broth, is it?" he asked about my chicken noodle soup after tasting a spoonful. "I can tell." Or he waved off spaghetti because, seeing the empty jar, declared, "I like the sauce you make from scratch better." He eschewed bottled dressing, choosing instead a Dijon vinaigrette he whisked himself in a stainless steel bowl. "Some balsamic vinegars are better than others," he intoned, or "Lobster without butter just isn't worth it." The capstone moment came when he asked me what was for dinner, and I said crab cakes.

"You know I don't like crab cakes," he groaned (I didn't know). "Can you make something else?"

"Like what?" I asked. He considered that a few moments.

"How about crab bisque?" he said. Bisque, I tell you. The kid was eleven. "Not for nothing," I replied, reaching for a seafood cookbook to accommodate my preteen's refining tastes, "but I was married before I even knew what bisque was."

So many of my precious memories revolved around moments like these with Joe and Ellie in the kitchen—laughing and talking as we chopped, stirred, tasted, created our signature dishes together, and shared a simple, lovingly prepared dinner. Good food, good smells, good times—"That's what we do," Ellie grinned.

Brad being gone so much necessarily forged a deep bond between the children and me. Looking back on their childhoods, my kids will remember long stretches of time with just the three of us in the picture, punctuated by brief, enthusiastic interludes with their father. I included them in the running of the household partly because I needed the help, but mostly to instill a sense of ownership, responsibility, and initiative about our family operations. I had no ego identification with being indispensable. Since toddlerhood Ellie and Joe were alongside me, under my tutelage, as I narrated the lessons of self-sufficiency. When they were little, I stocked a low kitchen cupboard with cereal, plastic bowls, and spoons so they could get their own breakfasts. There was a pint-sized container of milk in the refrigerator that they could pour without spilling. After eating, they put their dishes in the sink.

The naturally domestic Ellie was an eager apprentice. As a teenager, she decorated her own room and kept it neat as a pin. In her spare time, she taught herself sewing and quilting and loved to tend the vegetable and flower gardens.

Joe, a bit of a slob, was initially a hostile witness, but he even did his own laundry now, usually by dumping the entire hamper of jeans and t-shirts into one super-sized load, then leaving it in the washer for a day or two. After drying it, he set the basket of unfolded clothing in the center of his room and fished out a wrinkled outfit each morning. Dresser drawers were just a redundancy.

Joe felt burdened by these responsibilities, as I found out when we stopped at a gas station and asked him to refuel the car.

"I don't know how!" he whined.

"I'll give you directions," I said, handing him my debit card. "Swipe this. Use the diagram to show you how. Now answer the questions."

"Do you want a receipt?" he read.

"Yes, because I deduct it from my checking account. That's what a debit is. When you're done, put on the gas cap and turn it until it clicks a few times." I was feeling so smug about our teachable moment.

"You've got me pumping your gas and doing my own laundry," he muttered from the back seat. "What's next?"

I refused to raise a son who believed elfkins came at night, folded the laundry, restocked the refrigerator, and cleaned the house. Spoiled sons became helpless adults and rotten spouses. I had some friends who didn't know how to microwave water or make their own beds when they went to college. That was bizarre to me. My mother ran an equal opportunity household, so chores were always a part of my life.

Having two mostly independent children made me feel like I had turned the corner on mommyhood. I was getting my life back, able to leave them on their own for hours at a time without rushing home to meet the school bus. I reflected on that seismic shift while attending a women's conference at Fort Irwin, California, in the fall. I ached for the young mother next to me who had a newborn in a baby seat and a toddler on her lap while she ran the family readiness table. Her husband was deployed so she had complete responsibility for two young children at all times, without a break. The exhaustion and loneliness must settle into her bone marrow, I thought. Every simple errand like getting a gallon of milk at the shoppette involved loading babies into and out of the car in super slow motion. She seemed poised and rested on the day I met her though. Then again, who knew what went on behind the closed doors of her home? Perhaps she put her children down for naps and then repaired to the shower for her long, racking daily sob, a favorite coping tool of military wives. I was lucky to have older children who could look after themselves during deployment and it still didn't stop me from crying regularly in the shower.

Both Ellie and Joe were still in school when Brad departed in mid-June. In New England, the academic year started after Labor Day and didn't end until well into summer if they had snow days to make up. This was one of those years. The day after school let out in late June, I got a back-to-school flyer from Staples in the mail. Some of our friends in southern states had already enjoyed two months of break by then, but being so far north, the dependably beautiful warm weather didn't really start until late July anyway.

As a mother, I always thought summers were challenging. It wasn't natural for children to have so much free time, and we all functioned better with structure instead of improvising and shifting on the fly. When Ellie and Joe were younger, I filled their vacation days with swimming lessons, library story hours, picnics, play dates, and outings. This was different.

About the same time Brad left, both kids lost all interest in spending time with me. That left me with long stretches of time at home during which I faced distractions like shuffling shit, moving laundry up from the basement, and sweeping out the garage. I was unable to commit to anything involving large blocks of time because I had to remain on the ready. The funny thing about teens and tweens was they didn't want you around except when they wanted you, and then it was a hair-on-fire situation. "I need a ride to the pool!" "Come pick me up at Jack's!" "I'm already late!"

Ellie, fifteen, had her teenage pastimes, which usually involved staying out past my bedtime. We were dangerously close to the alarm clock technique, where she had to wake me up when she came home, and it had better be before curfew. Of course, if I had to pick her up, then she had to call it an early night. She also had a few new friends of a sinister,

Goth variety who creeped me out. When I asked what she did or where she'd been, she answered cryptically, "We watched a video in the Barraca's basement" or "We were just around town."

Joe was deep in preteen throes, interested only in time with the guys. Baseball took a big chunk of his life, as did other boy things like hanging out at the ball field concession stand, playing man hunt on summer nights, skateboarding to the local deli for French fries, and going to movies (the cinema had become a middle school hangout). In our small town, he and his crew were good old-fashioned free-range kids, probably the last of a dying breed.

If only for my sake, we had to impose a little structure on this lash up. Ellie and Joe loved their free time, and I supported "hanging out" as essential to a well-lived childhood and adolescence, but a two-month free-for-all wasn't going to work, not when I was a one-woman show.

Gradually I corralled my offspring and we evolved a plan for July and August. Ellie wanted to attend track and field camp at Providence College and art classes at Rhode Island School of Design. Joe would be busy with all-star baseball, followed by surf camp and sports camp, both local. I signed up for a stained glass class in town. We planned a hiking trip to New Hampshire with some family friends and a long Labor Day weekend at Cape Cod to finish off the summer. In addition, Joe was going to Indianapolis with me so I could attend my high school reunion, and from there he would fly by himself to Montana for two weeks at Grandma's with the male cousins who were his age. (We called the five of them "The Dingos" because of their preference for traveling in a pack like wild dogs.)

As for the remaining summer, we would fill it by making use of our beach passes and all the kayaking opportunities in beautiful southern Rhode Island. (It was often recognized as a top vacation spot, and we were lucky enough to live there.) Then autumn beckoned and we would be one-fourth of the way through deployment.

We all loved the eighteenth-century New England mill town where we lived. After renting for two years in a soporific, vinyl suburb on the outskirts, we bought a modest house within walking distance of the town center. Our immediate neighborhood was once a small farm that a developer had divided into five plots on an extended cul de sac. We lived at the entrance. Along my side yard, obscured behind a wall of evergreens, was a paved bike path that ran from the train station into town (nearly six miles), with plans to continue it another two miles to the beach. In the 1920s, it had been an ancillary rail route transporting moneyed New Yorkers from the main northeast corridor to the resort casino by the water. Today it snaked through our semirural area like a spool of thread unrolling past schools, creeks, and shops.

While some might object to a recreation path so close, I enjoyed every minute of it. For one thing, a peaceful walk, jog, or bike ride was right outside my door. On this "linear park," as it was called, I was always running into people I knew—friends training for a 10K or in-line skating.

For another, I was treated to an engaging stream of vitality as I worked in the yard or sat in my living room. Young mothers sauntered by pushing strollers and wrestling Labradors on leashes. A retired gentleman ambled past at a stately pace with his two herding dogs, which were so placid they looked lobotomized. My neighbor nicknamed him Mr. BOSM, for Bag of Shit Man, because he carried his plastic bag before him so reverently, as if it were a gift to the Messiah. A pack of cyclists in day-glow color-block jerseys whizzed by in a phalanx. The high school cross country team finishing their workout returned my wave. We once saw a businessman pedal up to the train station, take a suit coat out of his backpack, jump into it, and stride onto the platform to catch a train to Boston. These were the endearing slices of small town life I was treated to every day.

During elementary school, Joe characteristically rolled out of bed at 8 a.m. and half jogged to his classroom, arriving just before the morning bell at 8:30. My sophomore Ellie hopped on her bike and headed to the high school ten minutes away. The path was an expressway for them, providing access to attractions and neighborhoods in the area—and thus to their friends—on the interconnected trails.

This pedestrian-centered place suited me. I walked to the bakery, the library, or the YMCA and biked to the post office or, more ambitiously, to meet a friend for coffee at the marina. My bicycle had fenders and a detachable basket for groceries. On the slippery slope to all-out dorkdom, could a handlebar bell and streamers be far behind?

When Brad first showed me the little Cape Cod–style home, I was against buying it. "So small!" I said. "Fourteen hundred square feet!" After too many years living in cramped government quarters with postage stamp kitchens, I put my foot down. "We need some quality of life." But he brought his staff officer training to bear and worked up a detailed cost/benefit analysis of buying versus continuing in our larger rental. Then he took us all to look at the house again, so I could be unimpressed once more with the beige exterior, lack of landscaping, and faded orange shutters, after which we walked (down the bike path) to the pizza place for lunch. Sitting in the booth by the window watching town scenes play out, both kids became smitten with village life, and, seeing its obvious benefits to our family, I soon followed. We made an offer on the place the next day. It was one of the few times I actually thanked Brad for being so stubborn. I found that our home, while tiny, was efficiently laid out so we used every inch of it. We had space for everything and the size of the rooms was fine. Behind the garage was a bicycle shed that Brad and I rehabbed to be my writing studio. Only during some exceptionally long, snowy winters when the four of us were marooned inside the house did it feel cramped. Or maybe it was just cabin fever.

Established around 1800, our town had once been a prosperous New England mill town and was now a historic district. The textile mill still stood in the center of town in the path of a creek, and the road system spider-webbed around it. A municipal commission was in the process of re-purposing the sprawling mill complex into a mixed commercial/retail venue, and already a custom motorcycle shop, indoor soccer field, and craft brewery had expressed interest. The original mill owners, who must have pulled down some incredible profits in their day, also had a philanthropic bent because they built the town hall, library, preschool, original post office, and the recreation center known as "the Guild." That was where both kids had music lessons, I took an upholstery class, the civic band practiced, and the senior citizens did aerobics on Thursday mornings. Situated between the mill and the Guild was a bucolic green, complete with a stonework bridge crossing a babbling brook. On either side of the grassy park were tennis courts and a playground, all within easy walking distance of our home. This was the village life I always wanted and I loved it.

The long game of a twelve-month deployment dictated new disciplines, such as realistic expectations about what I could accomplish during my waking hours. I was a bit of a type-A fiend who routinely worked myself to a nub and didn't like to dial down because it felt like failing. I wasn't wired for self-care, especially if there was any suspicion on my part that I was inconveniencing my family. Then the guilt tape kicked in: "Don't be needy and don't be neurotic." These two restrictions kept me running at max capacity, fueled by caffeine and adrenaline, until I couldn't take another step.

A decade or so earlier, while Brad attended a two-month course in Kansas, he came back home to Virginia for Easter weekend. I don't remember much about his visit because I fell asleep on the couch Saturday morning and stayed there. Momentarily, I'd wake, lift my head to check on things, then fall back asleep until it was time to go to bed. My body said, "I'm done. Recovery starts now." For a month I'd looked after our petulant toddler (who still wasn't sleeping through the night) by myself, then collapsed when Brad came home. "Sorry I didn't spend much time with you this weekend," I apologized sheepishly as I drove him back to the airport on Sunday afternoon. But hey, at least I was rested.

The key was to pace myself by making better choices all along. In late summer, I took a quiz on the Internet about women's health and my results said I put severe demands on my body. "Put yourself first!" the article admonished. Easier said than done, I thought, especially when the opposite programming was ingrained in my head.

That same week, I was lacing up my shoes after a strenuous vinyasa class at the yoga studio when the instructor sat down beside me and studied my face. "How are you?" she asked, carefully smoothing aside the lock of hair matted to my sweaty forehead.

"I have good days and bad days," I said. "I'm getting run down."

"I can tell," she said. "Your kids don't know me from a hole in the ground, but I can hang out with them if it will give you a break. Remember what they tell you on airplanes. Put your own oxygen mask on first."

Put your own oxygen mask on first—but hypersensitivity to others was my primary focus, and the focus of most women around me, I noticed, as we waited for permission to take care of ourselves. A teacher at Joe's school suffered a nervous breakdown converging with physical problems from Lyme disease and was hospitalized for two weeks. On medical leave from work for four months, she outlined her doctor's dictates to me: "Exercise. Eat three meals a day. Cut out coffee. Sleep eight hours a night."

"In other words, take better care of yourself," I said.

"I waited until someone told me to do that," she admitted.

Janice, one of my neighbors from our early Army days, experienced depression after the birth of her first child. The doctor's "prescription" was for her to put the baby in child care three mornings a week and attend aerobics classes. Another attorney friend, classified with a high-risk pregnancy, had to be threatened with hospitalization by her obstetrician if she didn't cut her work week back to forty hours. Official medical orders were the only directive she (and her firm) would accept.

I routinely waited for Brad to tell me to take a break. Suffering from excessive altruism, I was protective of him, his time, his feelings, his career, and his sleep because he was the breadwinner, so even if I were just going to the YMCA, I made sure both kids were taken care of, dinner was simmering in the crock pot, and the table was set. With my elaborate preparations, no one had to be disturbed, but there were so many hoops to jump through that I rarely broke away.

When Brad wanted to go running, he just changed into his jogging clothes and left. He claimed his time; I negotiated for mine, and not even very assertively. "I can't think of a more powerless position to put yourself in," our marriage counselor advised me. "Always waiting for Brad to give the go-ahead."

Yet there I was in all my pathetic powerlessness, looking to my husband for support and reassurance, forgetting as usual that they were alien concepts to him.

I believed paying attention to my needs was selfish and unraveling this restriction was difficult. "Any little bit of experimenting in self-nurturance is very frightening for most of us," writing coach Julie Cameron has said. Eventually, I reached such a frazzled state—enlightenment at gunpoint—that I had to design healthy guidelines and carry them out as if they were orders.

GO TO BED EARLY

While hanging out at the beach with Ellie and Joe one summer day, I devoured a novel by favorite author Edith Wharton—*The Buccaneers*.

This would make a great movie, I kept thinking, and finally spoke it out loud. "It's already a miniseries," my neighbor said. "They filmed part of it in Newport." An Internet check of the library database revealed they had the eight-episode DVD series, so I checked it out and stayed up so late watching it, I could barely keep my eyes open. Then I straggled off to bed without washing my face or brushing my teeth.

The next day I was irritable and in a brain fog. Bitterly tired, I snapped at Joe as we loaded the car for baseball. "I'm sorry," he said, blaming himself entirely. "I'm *so* sorry." Later I apologized to him for being short-tempered and assured him it wasn't his fault. But you can't unring a bell.

There were some behaviors, I realized, I could not engage in during deployments, like staying up late channel or Internet surfing. This wasn't business as usual anymore. Without sufficient sleep, I was in poor form for the family, and no other adult could pick up the slack for me the next day. I became ineffective, mercurial, and unable to remember things or form complete sentences. More and more often, while waiting in the car during guitar or baseball practice, I reclined the seat and fell asleep instantly. Most nights I collapsed into bed, trembling with exhaustion.

The first time Brad deployed, a wise military wife advised me to "go to bed when the kids go to bed." Because they were both in elementary school at the time, the three of us shut down the house together not long after the dinner dishes were done and went upstairs. My lengthy and much-loved ritual with them involved lying in bed with each child reading books, then reflecting on the day, or "talk what we did," as Ellie called it. I didn't go back downstairs afterward, as was my wont, but went to the master bedroom where I took a bubble bath, gave myself a manicure, or just picked up a novel until I turned off the light and fell asleep, which under this routine, was fairly early.

With older children during the Afghanistan deployment, I got into the habit of returning to the family room after tucking in Ellie and Joe. Pasted to the couch, I flipped through cable channels endlessly or got involved in some mediocre B movie until it was so late I could hardly drag myself to bed.

This behavior had to stop. I forced myself to turn off all electronics at 9 p.m. and started the going to bed motions. As any mother knew, there were impediments along the way such as delivering folded laundry to bureau drawers, signing permission slips, and starting the dish-washer. I still made it into my pajamas at a decent hour instead of burning the midnight oil web surfing or other nonsense that left me too tired to function the next day.

SPECIAL MEASURES

All my life, I've been a world-class sleeper—when my head hit the pillow, I slipped into a coma and stayed there all night. It was my super power.

During Brad's absence, I began experiencing fitful, restless nights punctuated with disturbing dream fragments. Always before, one good night's sleep set me back to zero. But now, even on the rare occasion when I got it, I still woke up tired. I feared I was back sliding so much I would never recover.

During an appointment for a routine physical, I explained the situation to the sympathetic Navy doctor. (Supposedly our assigned practitioner but I'd never seen him before—typical of military life. Our family doctor was whoever had an open appointment at the clinic.) Husband deployed, two kids, a job. After five years of war by then, the doctors could spot problems and tease out the underlying truths.

"I'm very tired and I can't seem to recover, even after a good night's sleep," I finally confessed, weariness written on my face and slumped posture.

"Is it anxiety?" he asked.

"Possibly," I said. The cumulative effects of many low-grade anxious moments throughout each day, each week, each month.

"I'll put in a prescription for Xanax," he said, punching the order into his laptop. "Don't take it every night. Just when you really need it."

And with that I joined the legion of stressed-out military wives on antidepressants or antianxiety medications. Legend had it that Army physicians handed these things out like candy. I've heard the urban myth that at the end of an appointment, the doctor casually asked his patient if she wanted her Prozac prescription refilled.

"Only thing was," the woman said, "I've never taken Prozac," and a simple check of her medical record would have confirmed that. The doctor just assumed drugs were standard issue for military wives. When we lived on post, almost all my neighbors took them.

I avoided medication, but I jumped at the chance for a small measure of relief. During my first night of sound sleep courtesy of Xanax, the Zamboni of my soul appeared, filling in the fractures in my psyche and restoring me to a pristine, rested state. The effect was dramatic and lasting. Only weeks later did I reach for the drug again when stress and fatigue brought me to the brink.

"Ah, yes, 'Sleep that knits up the ravell'd sleeve of care,'" I quoted Shakespeare as I knocked back one of the little pills and shuffled to bed. My orange pharmacy bottle, still half full when Brad got home, stood in the back of the medicine cabinet as a sentry of sanity for the rest of the year.

MAKING TIME FOR REGULAR EXERCISE

With my vigorous physical energy, I needed this outlet, and if I didn't get it, I became like a caged animal. Even Joe and Ellie said to me from time to time, "You're grouchy. You need to go for a walk." Bicycling and walking were easy to do with the recreation path right beside our house. If it snowed, I laced up boots and hiked in the woods behind us. During the school year, our routine became for me to drop Ellie off at 7:30 p.m., then drive to the beach for an off-season walk. By 9 a.m., I was finished and headed home for a shower.

Yoga was trickier because I needed a large block of time in my schedule—easily two hours—to take a class. When things got busy, it was an elective I easily threw overboard to make room for a family demand. Yoga was the first thing I let go of and it should have been the last. I had to put my own oxygen mask on first, like the instructor said. "Oxygen mask, oxygen mask" became the mantra as I showed up at the yoga studio, repeating it silently to drown out the litany of chores coursing through my brain.

DRINKING ALCOHOL

There were some behaviors I could no longer indulge in, and drinking was one of them. The blood and brain chemistry changes of my mid-forties meant the wine or martinis I once easily consumed in social situations became difficult to metabolize. I wasn't sharp the next morning or I bolted upright at 3 a.m., unable to fall back asleep. Then for the rest of the day, I was depleted and sad, a harsh reminder that the momentary escape of alcohol just wasn't worth it.

But boy, when I hit the mind-numbing grind of mid-deployment, the prospect of belting back a few sturdy shots of gin and sliding into unconsciousness sounded tempting—I won't lie. In the immediate aftermath of 9/11, I watched too many horrific images of planes flying into buildings and then numbed out with a glass of chardonnay. It felt so good I had another, and another, until I woke up at dawn on the couch with the empty bottle beside me. Believe me, it wasn't a pretty look.

There was no one around now to pick up the slack while I nursed a hangover. No partner who could let me sleep it off, make the pancakes for breakfast, and shuttle Joe to soccer. It was all single, solitary, and—necessarily—sober me.

SERENITY SPOTS

A well-run home was my solace and where I wanted to be, but getting it to that point was often a futile exercise. Housekeeping has been compared to shoveling the sidewalk while it's still snowing or loading beads on a string with no knot at the end. Every mother knew the endless drill of straightening up the downstairs, only to find it trashed the next day.

In our house, most of the arriving took place at the back door. We entered a mudroom where we dropped our bags, backpacks, coats, and shoes, then proceeded into the kitchen. After a few steps, I normally stopped and began loading dirty glasses and bowls into the dishwasher. I spent so much time in front of the kitchen sink it was like a sand trap or a bramble patch. Pausing to put a few things away led to starting dinner, which I did while Joe sat at the breakfast bar doing homework. Ellie wandered down the short hallway to her bedroom—the Opium

Den as we called it due to the boho-chic burgundy and pea green walls, her brass elephant collection, and predilection for batik.

The kitchen-mudroom-dining room was heavily trafficked and had to be cleaned often. Everywhere there were clothes to pick up, mail to sort, phone messages, dust piles, team schedules, coupons, plants needing water, overflowing trash cans, stacks, or spider webs dangling from the soffit. The situation came unglued even as I moved around tending to it.

"Nothing adds up," my friend Robin once said about life with her two toddlers. "But here's the thing," she continued. "I learned if I cleaned my bedroom first, it stayed nice. Then I always had a place to go for a break."

I remembered an uptight college friend once spoke with a professional counselor about her anxiety. The therapist suggested she make a list of comfort spots around campus, places where she could sit for a while and feel calmer—the walking path in the green was one, the sundial garden or the bench by the pond were others, the art museum another. They became restorative spaces for her.

I created my own serenity spot rule. Because my home represented work to me, I found it impossible to relax there. Yet that's where I needed to be because it was the locus of our life. In order to be present without being stressed out, I needed to discover sanctuaries in my own house.

One was my small, uncluttered bedroom—freshly dusted with a fluffy duvet, yummy feather pillows, neatly folded throw, and a novel on the bedside table. While in the restful embrace of my room—the essence of simplicity—all was well with the world.

Another spot was our living room, which was rarely used because most of the action took place on the opposite side of the house. Our cozy sitting room was decorated enough to feel inviting but not overwhelmingly fussy. It stayed neat because only Ellie went in there to play the piano, and before long that's where I migrated for a moment's solitude and centering with my cup of tea and a magazine.

When weather allowed, we had a fantastic back deck. A courtyard, I called it, but my mom corrected me: "a lanai," she said, pointing out it was enclosed by three walls. It was the sheltered space between the house and the detached garage immediately behind us, a protected outdoor room with views of the sky and trees. I had fixed it up with trellises for privacy from cul de sac traffic and window boxes spilling with coleus and deep purple petunias. In the summers we often ate candlelight dinners out there, and I found afternoon peace in the red-wood recliners among the breezes and birdsong.

Finally, I had what Virginia Woolf advocated: "a room of one's own." Across the driveway and behind the garage was an unused garden shed. Brad and I had removed the random shovels and rakes and swept it clean of spiders. "This will be my writing room," I declared. Fortunately it had one window and a line of electricity from the garage. Brad insulated it, installed a dropped ceiling, and nailed up bead board. We painted the walls a soft mint and laid down a Berber carpet remnant. It was just a small, standard shed, but it was all I needed. On one wall I put a secondhand desk for my computer and printer. The opposite side had a small table, and just to the left of the doorway there was enough room for a bookcase. Because there was only a bare bulb with a string hanging from it, I had to get some task lighting. In the winter, a space heater kept me warm. Summer afternoons were too hot in there, but if I confined my work time to mornings or evenings, I was fine, especially after I attached an instant screen door that allowed a breeze and kept out the bugs (and occasionally skunks!). It was spare and Spartan, but it served as a threshold to a place devoted entirely to my writing in a way that a corner of the dining room table couldn't. Now, what to call it? These days, they have a snappy term—"She Sheds"—but back then I thought of it as my writing studio. Joe called it "mom's clubhouse" and Ellie said it was my "cubby." From its inception, Brad called it my "hooch" (after the Asian hut, because he spent a year in Korea as a lieutenant), and that's what it became. When we got a yellow lab puppy, she slept under my desk and became the "hooch pooch." That's where I wrote my first and second books, pitched articles, revised manuscripts, and brainstormed essay ideas. Tucked away in there, I was technically still home, but undisturbed and undistracted, which allowed my creativity to blossom.

ENDING MY LOVE AFFAIR WITH TYPE-A WOMEN

This was more of a tangle. My kids already had to go through so much emotionally with their father gone that I tried to say "Yes" to them as much as possible to make up for his lack. The guilt gene operated on warp speed.

Yes, you can play fall baseball. Yes, I'll take you to another neighborhood to play flashlight tag with your friends after dark. Yes, I'll drive you to the beach *and* pick you up at the end of the day. Yes, even if it meant more demands on me, to the point of exhaustion. They had their own lives, but I remained available to provide logistical support. I assigned myself permanent on-call status.

Realistically, I couldn't provide the services of two parents, but the notion dovetailed nicely with my lifelong habit of overextending myself. My tendency to pack my schedule, to overzealously accept, and to be the first to step up prompted a friend to observe, "You have two speeds: urgent and super white hot urgent." Was I—gasp—a stress junkie? Every morning I attacked a list of obligations that filled a legal-sized paper and hustled full tilt boogie all day, sometimes doing two or three things at once, until I crashed after dinner, unable to limp upstairs. But even in my martyrdom, I felt self-important and accomplished. There was always a striving and straining in me, even in yoga class where I pushed through the postures with jaw-clenching intensity.

This deployment held up an unrelenting mirror to my entrenched behavior, which by now had reached epic proportions. My mind was the city that never slept. If I didn't pull the plug, my overworked circuits were going to explode. I couldn't justify my habits anymore when they had such a detrimental effect on my well-being.

I tried to break up with the type-A woman, but she stalked me relentlessly. At the first hint of downsizing, the leering internal admonition to "Go Go Go" redoubled its efforts. I had a strong, almost impenetrable ego attachment to being the "woman who got shit done." When it became obvious that she and I couldn't coexist, there was going to be a battle royale. This year gave me an opportunity to examine the deep psychological underpinnings of that conflict, and so many others, at great emotional cost.

In southern Rhode Island, we were hundreds of miles from a divisional Army post like Fort Bragg or Fort Stewart. That made us quite the anomaly as the lone military family in a largely civilian area. While across the bay there was a Navy base, aside from the serendipitous and rare reconnection with Army friends who cycled through the Naval War

College, we didn't do much there except commissary shop and visit the doctor. That left me without the familiar structure of a military town, like friends in close quarters who also had deployed husbands and who were ever ready to get together for pizza or an impromptu potluck.

I've made my share of emergency trips to a fellow military wife who needed a helping hand during distress—times when her father was hospitalized with a stroke and her husband was in the thick of things in Fallujah, for example. Sometimes it was only to feed her little ones dinner so she could chain smoke on the back porch and have a long, uninterrupted phone conversation with her mother. Similarly, when my grandmother died, Brad was in Kosovo, and I, lonely and tired, faltered under the grief. Somehow the wives' grapevine heard and mobilized, checking on me, calling, stopping by, bringing dinner, inviting me out, and offering to babysit or pick up the kids from soccer. They knew just what I needed—some adult company, a shoulder to cry on, and a life-line back to shallow water.

I didn't have that culture of proactive empathy and teamwork here. But the flip side of the coin was that in a military town, everyone was as dogged out as me. It was difficult to ask for help from someone who faced the same withering challenges as I did every day. Those conditions also engendered a "suck-it-up mob" culture that worked well until it didn't, and then it failed spectacularly. At least in Rhode Island, my circle of friends would be fresh and, I hoped, eager to help.

The week after Brad left, Sue invited me out for breakfast with some other moms. We had the best breakfast places in southern Rhode Island—mom and pop spots with nostalgic lunch counters, mismatched chairs, bottomless cups of coffee, and gum-snapping waitresses who greeted you with a hearty, "Where ya been? Haven't seen ya in a long time."

As I tore into my platter of bacon and French toast drowning in maple syrup, talk turned to Brad and Afghanistan. Sue let out a long sigh as she reflected, "It's personal now. I know someone over there." The two other women at the table were also quiet for a few moments. After five years of war, it had finally touched their lives.

Brad asked me to keep track of how people helped because he wanted to thank them—"catch 'em doing something right"—so I dutifully recorded whenever anyone did something thoughtful. The list of kindnesses grew.

My neighbor, a Vietnam veteran in his late sixties, carried his extension ladder over in the fall and said, "I noticed your gutters need cleaning. Mind if I just take care of it right now?"

Neighbors Magda and Rick looked after my two children while I attended a family funeral in New York City. They also picked them up from guitar lessons when I couldn't and loaned me their extra car when mine died.

My friend Cindy offered to shuttle Joe to baseball practice and games, and because of her attentiveness in many other ways, our friendship deepened and grew that year. Angie, mother of the twins, gave Joe a ride to middle school every day (where she worked) and invited us to Easter dinner at her house. Holly took me away for a much-needed overnight at Block Island to decompress and rest in August. Patricia called often to check on me and invited me out for drinks from time to time. Sue was my faithful and ever ready walking partner.

The in-laws in Virginia Beach invited us down for Thanksgiving and even paid for half the airline tickets. My mother watched my kids when I went out of town on business in the fall, and my two sisters in California rolled out the red carpet for us at Christmas. Joe's best friend included him on their annual family vacation to Maine, where they stayed in rustic lake cabins and water skied, making wonderful lifetime memories together.

My hen party at the Little League games—single mothers all—kept up my spirits with their gossip and lively companionship during long afternoons on the bleachers.

There were other gestures too: Ellie took a CD of photographs to the photo store to make prints and when the manager saw they were of her father in Afghanistan, he didn't charge her. The president of the local university invited us to watch football and basketball games in the VIP suite. The dean of students, whom Brad had worked with, called the house once a month to see how we were doing. Our monthly fee was waived at the YMCA during the deployment. The town florist started saving boxes for me after she saw me fishing some out of her dumpster and I explained I needed them for care packages to my husband in Afghanistan. "Tell him thank you," she always added when I picked up a batch. One afternoon, a friend showed up at the door holding a pan of homemade lasagna. "Just heat this up for thirty minutes at 350 degrees," she smiled. "I wanted you to have a break tonight." Who knew the classic, unbidden kindness of a covered dish could bring me to tears?

In the past I'd been on the receiving end of "virtue signalers," people who parroted the platitude, "If there's anything I can do to help, let me know," only to repeatedly turn down my requests with lame excuses like "I can't. I'm pushing back my cuticles that evening. It's the only time I can do it. But really, any other time. Happy to help." In reality, they never wanted to be inconvenienced. This year was different. So many thoughtful people looked out for the lone military family in their midst. When they reached out with the smallest gestures—a message left on voicemail, some cut flowers in a jelly jar, an invitation to coffee, generosity to my children—it lightened my burden, eased my loneliness, and fortified me. I went through several packages of thank you notes acknowledging them, but the outpouring was so abundant, I couldn't keep up. I hope they understood how much it meant.

"I don't really miss dad yet. He's only been gone a few days," Joe said offhandedly at breakfast. I'd been observing him and his sister closely (but unobtrusively) for telltale behaviors indicating problems. So far I'd seen nothing. This wasn't their first rodeo—they were military kids through and through. Besides knowing what to do when retreat sounded (even if they were in the middle of soccer practice), and what "quarters" and "oh-dark-thirty" were, it also meant Dad went away a lot, sometimes for months, while we carried on as usual. He returned to great fanfare and hand-painted signs.

While Joe and Ellie seemed resilient and well-adjusted, sometimes the weight and balance shifted unexpectedly and a fissure opened. For example, the heartbreaking memory of Joe as a kindergartner, jumping out of bed and running down two flights of stairs at five in the morning. He'd heard the garage door opening and suddenly wanted nothing more than to say goodbye to his Dad, who was leaving for a few weeks. What did Brad think, I wondered, when he glimpsed through the windshield his five-year-old boy in Toy Story pajamas, scrambling down the basement steps with a panicked look on his face, desperate for one last embrace? I followed Joe downstairs in my nightgown, gathered him up after his Daddy hug, carried him back to bed, and curled around him protectively until he fell back asleep. I was not so fortunate. The scene had been so wrenching that I tossed and turned until the alarm rang.

My kids didn't articulate succinctly what was bothering them, such as, "I'm feeling a little sad about Dad being gone. I'd like to schedule some time to talk to you about it." Knotholes revealed themselves in subtle and spontaneous ways. As I worked on my laptop in the dining room one evening, Ellie walked in and asked if I would come say good-night. Sleepy and undefended, she lay back on her pillow. "I miss Dad," she offered quietly. Her soulful eyes, hazel and paisley shaped—so like Brad's—blinked back tears. I lingered with her a long time, smoothing her thick blonde hair, offering words of comfort and reassurance. There was nothing else I could do except be present.

Home was the three of us—Ellie, Joe, and me. I wanted them to believe completely in my constancy and love. I tried with imperfect results to make up for the man-sized hole in their lives where their father should be and where a husband should be for me.

At the end of each day I crawled into bed alone, the ponderous sadness pressing in on me from all directions. I hadn't imagined marriage could be so lonely. With no nightly nurturing or shoulder to sleep on or warm body nearby, my cherished notions of a close emotional partnership with Brad were growing ever more distant and unrecognizable.

4

COMMUNICATION, TELECOMMUNICATION, AND MISCOMMUNICATION

Functioning separately was factory installed into the operating system of our marriage. Brad was training in Jordan with his Ranger unit until several weeks before our wedding. Not long after we married, he moved to a different post to attend a career course. He missed much of Ellie's first year because he was commanding an infantry company, and in the absence of person-to-person interaction, we were forced to use alternative methods to stay close.

We've lived through a sea change as far as modes of communication went. When Brad and I started out on this journey in 1989, letters and print photographs were the main ways to stay in touch during long field exercises, unaccompanied tours, and the rare four- to six-month deployments. Many times when Brad was out training for several weeks, there was no communication at all. This was also something I got used to.

When I was in Honduras for four months (before I married Brad), Internet and e-mail weren't invented yet. We were allotted two free fifteen-minute calls home each week. I joined the queue outside the only morale-and-welfare phone, and when it was my turn, I sat inside the hot, grimy, mosquito-infested plywood booth while those waiting eyed me impatiently and looked at their watches.

It's difficult to believe, but during a deployment to Central America, the wife of a soldier had a baby and the command didn't let him go home for the birth, even though it was only a four-hour flight. We've become more family-friendly since then and deployments are now long-er and more frequent, so adjustments had to be made.

Video cameras were just coming into vogue then, but they were expensive, unwieldy, and as big as briefcases. Sometime in the late 1990s when Brad was in the Balkans, we filmed videos and shipped them to him (yes, video cartridges, not DVDs—those came later). Shooting it was a big production and took several weeks.

Through the years cameras have scaled down so much that they're now a part of the cell phone. These days everyone has smartphones that, in a space the size of an index card, contain functions previously requiring a roomful of gadgets—telephone, answering machine, computer, stereo, still photo camera, radio, video camera, and tape recorder. And with the phone in your pocket or purse, you're immediately available, even if you're walking the aisles at the grocery store. (I can't tell you how many times I used up my fifteen-minute morale call dialing family members and getting answering machines.)

Now there's a dizzying array of up-to-the-minute communication options. Military families can text, Tweet, or Instagram one another in addition to Skype, Facetime, or Google Hangouts. I'm still amazed that we can now send photographs via e-mail. No more taking the roll of film to the developer, waiting for photos, and ordering extra prints of the best ones to share by snail mail. I realize this wasn't the most cutting-edge innovation, but it still thrills me. Remember, I thought it was high tech when telephones became cordless.

When Brad went to Afghanistan in 2006, the culture was not yet fluent in social media. E-mail and cell phones were available, but operational security and policy precluded using too much Internet during deployments. Brad sent me a Department of Defense PowerPoint slide show about the dangers of posting too much information on Facebook, particularly by wives of deployed soldiers who put their personal safety at risk. The example they easily pulled off the Internet (with relevant names and faces blurred out) was the time line of a young mother who shared that her husband was deployed and she was home alone with a little baby. The status updates also gave her full name, the city and state where she lived, pictures of her house, and the license plate number on her car. "Be careful about this," he warned me.

Skype was fairly new, but we opted against it. Our parenting strategy was to "put Dad on the shelf and take him down every now and then to check the expiration date." This coping system had worked for us in the past. It was amazing how resilient the kids were after a short adjustment period. Skype or teleconferencing undermined it by bringing virtual images of Dad front and center, reminding them of how much they missed him. "Out of sight, out of mind" worked better.

E-mail offered the best option for up-to-the minute news, but with limitations. It changed our discourse into banal, bulleted, efficiently packaged information, like a telegram. Stop. But e-mail was better than enduring long intervals between phone calls and letters as we had in the past. By exchanging a minimum daily dose of logistical sound bites, we managed to keep the arc of communication alive, even if the contents were often factoids containing little reflection or sentiment.

> *Joe stayed home from school today for a doctor's appointment. He had a wart on his knee frozen off.*
> *Ellie reports learning a lot at javelin camp. She wants to get her own javelin now—even more than she wants a new bike.*
> *Joe got picked for all stars.*
> *These pictures were taken at Joe's graduation. It was a Hawaii-themed ceremony, as you can see.*
> *Ellie is going to volunteer for the Land Trust doing conservation work this summer.*
> *Today I went to watch U.S. Open golf in Newport. Waited a couple of hours for the fog to clear but ended up leaving without seeing anyone swing a club.*
> *Ellie and I tried to install the CD player today. We couldn't get the computer to recognize the drive. Finally, a friend of hers came over and figured it out for us.*
> *I bought a bunch of perennials at the master gardener sale.*
> *We spent the morning having an enjoyable muffin breakfast on the deck. Ellie has been studying all afternoon.*
> *Joe is at practice and Ellie and I were thinking about going to get a scoop of ice cream.*
> *Paid bills this morning then mailed a package to you.*
> *We got a form from the church saying we didn't turn in a completed sponsor form for confirmation. What should I do?*

Brad's were equally *pro forma*:

Feel like I might be coming down with something. Need to be careful.
Don't have time to be sick.
Been feeling the crunch the last couple weeks of being understaffed.
The three officers on the team are currently doing the work of at least
six officers.
I've been very busy, none of it "make work." Job is most satisfying.

We also discovered we could have cyber arguments that escalated fairly quickly if we weren't careful. Something about having a keyboard at your fingertips instead of a human in front of you emboldened commentary. One day I came home to find this phone message: "I'm sorry. I'm doing pushups for you. Love, Brad."

Despite my lingering resentment over our exchange, I couldn't help but smile. Earlier that day, he'd sent me this cold e-mail: "I tried accessing our USAA account for the first time since leave. The PIN has changed. Couldn't get in. Failed several times calling you today."

It was my fault. Our bank had recently instituted a PIN as a second layer of security and I'd forgotten to mention it to Brad. Now if I'd been in patient wifely form, I would've recognized his tone as that of someone who was only tired and frustrated, not confrontational, and I could have easily defused the situation. That didn't happen. My equally incendiary response was "USAA upped their security. That's the reason for the change in access. May I suggest you not worry about the account but trust me as you so often say you do."

He fired another salvo: "$1,000 to the Citizen's account. What's the point of transferring that much money? I just noticed you made reservations for the reunion in Texas. That's a change since our last conversation."

So he had been going through the bank statements with a fine-toothed comb? I flashed back to him balancing the checkbook early in our marriage and muttering, "All these things you bought." Right, wild expenditures like paper towels, tissues, socks, diapers, milk, and ground beef, I thought. Everything he touched in our house was purchased by me so of course I spent more money than he did. It was a button—then and now.

"I slid the $1,000 into savings," I replied, "out of the checking account where it will just get pissed away. We might as well have a nest egg when this year's over. Quit being Big Brother."

Fortunately, we both had the good sense to withdraw at that point before one of us went nuclear. Sometime later when we'd both rested and eaten something, he left the contrite phone message about doing pushups for me. I apologized for neglecting to tell him the new PIN and for forgetting that he also had his own USAA checking account he needed to monitor.

Crisis averted—this time—but there were many other times when the demands of daily life and distance spun into messy cyber squalls. It certainly wasn't the way we wanted to spend our limited communication time.

When Brad deployed to Kosovo in 2000, I wrote him an e-mail every day, sometimes more often, just to keep him up to date on home matters and the children. I didn't send him any letters. Not long after he got home, his commander mentioned that he received "twenty-seven cards" from his wife while he was gone for six months.

"He got twenty-seven cards and I didn't send you any," I mewled apologetically. After a pause, Brad said, "That's okay. I knew you were really busy." But I could tell it bothered him.

To his point, the couple in question had no children, so their situation was different. The other consideration was that I believed that e-mails were interchangeable with letters. They weren't. The truth is, I would have been happy to send him cards and letters now and then. I flashed to the summer camp memory of repairing to my bunk for rest time after lunch, anticipating the thrill of hearing my name called as the counselor handed out letters from home. It was more than a message from Mom—it was bonding, attention, acknowledgment, and remembrance, all in recognizable handwriting, the reading of which (and perhaps rereading) would be precious.

Brad and I had never talked about our preferred method of communication or even the desired frequency. I just assumed e-mails exclusively would be fine with him. He actually longed for something more personal. E-mails were a single syllable when one craved a paragraph. One was soft-serve, the other hand-dipped, French vanilla ice cream from a local dairy topped with homemade hot fudge and whipped cream.

From then on, we understood that letter writing complemented our frequent e-mails and took connection to the next level, as Brad often emphasized when he closed his e-mails with—"I'll write you a real letter tonight."

I sat on the back deck on a summer morning not long after Brad departed, savoring the time while I was the only one stirring—our two babies still slept peacefully. I'd already finished one cup of coffee, so I refilled my mug, grabbed a notepad and pen, and went back outside to write Brad a letter. I made it a point to write him an actual letter once a week, in addition to sending him the daily "here's what's up" e-mails. I imagined some of the good vibes from this perishable moment wending their way into my words and sentiments. "I'm outside enjoying this beautiful, sunny day. The birds are twittering away in the trees and there's a sweet, warm breeze. You know how mornings in New England are before summer officially kicks in (sometime in August!)."

Letters captured these elements of place, pause, and reflection. "We are easing into summer," I continued. "The kids are decompressing from the daily treadmill of early wakeups and full days of school and other demands. Both are sleeping in. I don't know what we'll do today. Yesterday I bought beach passes so maybe we'll head there later." I cherished the thought that I was imparting a little of the family's mood and tone to him, even though he was six thousand miles away. He wasn't a visual person, but I pictured him being momentarily transported in mind and spirit to our salt box home, tall trees rustling in the yard, early morning bikers pedaling past, and out on the patio, his wife working on correspondence.

When I put a pen in my hand, it accessed a stockpile of visceral images, activating an emotional reservoir of which I was only vaguely conscious in my daily life. Someone else took over, a persona who had been quietly recording sensations, a scribe intent on meticulously rendered vignettes infused with meaning for her husband far away. They came from a softer, deeper, more affectionate space than e-mails typed between washing the car and taking out the garbage. Letters gave us a reassuring sense of reconnection, a timeless, distanceless, crystallized moment. Research shows that different areas of the brain are stimulated when writing longhand versus when using the keyboard. What synapses fired in me? Mushy, poetic, mindful ones, I thought. "The letter is truly a unique form of communication that loses intimacy when done digitally," Brad wrote to me from California in 2002. Yes—it was more intimate. The act of drawing a pen across a clean white sheet of paper resulted in more revealing and humanizing contact.

During the Afghanistan deployment, I wrote letters regularly to boost his morale. Instead of electronic e-mails on a server, the epistolary record of our times apart would be a stack of hand-addressed, postmarked envelopes tied with grosgrain ribbon and tucked in a scented bureau drawer, to be taken out occasionally and reread on leisurely afternoons.

One should never underestimate the morale-building effect of a gift from home. During a deployment to the Balkans in 2000, one of the soldiers in Brad's unit returned to Fort Campbell briefly and offered to deliver packages back to Kosovo. We made Brad a batch of chocolate chip cookies and a hand-drawn construction paper card, which then traveled in his buddy's duffel bag back overseas.

"I swear those cookies were still warm when I got them," Brad gushed. "Thank you SO much." It was the surprise and the tender loving care that made such an impact.

This time I wanted to proactively put a system in place for care packages, so we placed a box next to the wall in the breakfast room. It was a fairly small container—the aisles of the local drug store were clogged with them on Tuesdays when they restocked the shampoo shelves. We dubbed it "The Dad Box," and inside were items we wanted to send to Brad. It was an ongoing collection point, for one thing, but with the big black Sharpie lettering on the inside flap, "For Dad," it also served as a daily reminder of him. The Dad Box was his presence in the heart of the home when we ate our bagels in the morning and when we reconvened for dinner.

"Let's put it in the Dad Box," I often said, referring to anything I wanted to share with Brad or thought he would love to see—copies of the children's report cards, school pictures, a coffee mug decorated with photographs of us, or a calendar of lovely Rhode Island scenes. We kept a regular care package process going and shipping the "Dad Box" became part of my routine.

When the box was nearly full, I emptied the contents on the dining room table to organize it and fill out the U.S. Customs form. For the last couple of weeks, I'd been placing items in this box as the ideas popped into my head, in much the same way as I'd stack things by the door in preparation for a family vacation. Brad got accustomed to receiving packages at frequent intervals so he knew if he asked for something, it would arrive forthwith. This one I prepared was heavy with items he'd requested: a jar of multivitamins, shoe orthotics from the sports store, all the remaining Army PT shorts from his bureau drawer, and five copies of my book, *Household Baggage*, which he'd been handing out to colleagues.

Then there were the personalized things I included so he knew we'd been thinking about him, like some clippings I'd saved: an article about Senator Reed's wife expecting a baby (our senator from Rhode Island, an Army Veteran, had visited Afghanistan and made a point of checking in with Brad); a lengthy and heartbreaking obituary of a young Marine from Warwick, Rhode Island, who died in Iraq. (Folks in Rhode Island were endearingly proprietary about anyone from their state, whether a contestant in the Miss America pageant or a singer on *American Idol*. He or she garnered front-page news coverage and the whole population got involved. It was a small state and instead of six degrees of separation, there was half a degree.) I added an article from *Southern Living* about the team who decorated Cracker Barrel restaurants and how all those plows and vintage oatmeal tins were obtained. This was a private joke because whenever we traveled, I insisted we eat every meal at Cracker Barrel. I loved fried catfish dipped in ketchup with a side of hashbrown casserole. Finally, I included the latest videos of the television series *Prison Break* we recorded for him (we had all gotten into it before he left), a list of suggestions for Christmas gifts, the program from the school play in which Joe had a small part, and any personal mail for him.

The last thing that went into each care package was the pages from a spiral notebook on the kitchen island. I kept it there for two reasons: one, to write down things that I wanted to talk to Brad about when he called; and two, for all of us to write daily notes to him or on the spur of the moment as the spirit moved us. Not quite a letter, but more personal than an e-mail, I thought. For example, Ellie once wrote, "I made a huge papier maché horse and painted it purple. It has tennis balls for hooves. My teacher put it on display in the library." Joe mentioned the skate park he fabricated in the driveway made of odds and ends from the garage (like Brad's West Point foot locker). I recounted something that happened at work. Each child wrote Brad every week and if they hadn't done it yet, these comments became their letter. I tore off these pages from the spiral notebook, trimmed the ragged, shedding edge, and laid them on top of the pile.

Then I wrapped and packed everything carefully, filled in the extra spaces with balled-up newspaper, and secured the package for the long trip to Afghanistan using, as Brad wryly noted, so much tape that he needed the Jaws of Life to open it.

I immediately replaced the departing Dad Box with an empty one, and we started putting together more gifts for our deployed soldier. This one was earmarked as a Christmas care package. To start off, I put one of our window wreaths in there, a spool of red velvet ribbon to staple Christmas cards to like we did at home, some CDs of holiday music, including Handel's *Messiah*, which he loved, and a beautiful bowl handmade by Ellie in her pottery class. More taped episodes of *Prison Break* would go in there, along with blank Christmas cards. We'd keep adding, and in several weeks, I'd take it to the post office. I was getting so good at filling out customs forms that I could do it with my eyes closed. In fact, I kept a stack of blank ones at my desk.

One day I arrived at home to find Joe on the phone with Brad. This situation was fraught with problems because Joe, who was watching television while he talked, got preoccupied with the show, and forgot he was in the middle of a conversation with Dad. Such was the attention span of our easily distracted twelve-year-old.

Brad demanded Joe hand the phone to me. I reluctantly took it. Even on great days, Brad and I were only marginally effective on the phone. International calls were doubly difficult because of the iffy connection, echo, feedback, and three-second delay. We accidentally interrupted each other repeatedly, with the resulting conversation so discombobulated that it was almost pointless. This time Brad talked most of the time. When I finally got to say something, he stepped on me. "Talk and then listen," I reminded him. I wished we'd remembered radio protocol from my Army days—say something, followed by "over." The other person waited before responding, also ending with "over." In a slow-motion, Ping-Pong parody, we'd have a conversation that was functional, but not fun.

We got cut off twice that day. The third time he called, I let the machine pick it up.

He always seemed to call at the wrong times. There was probably never a convenient time because household activities continued full bore and I had demands facing me all the time. If I were home, I was putting out fires or preparing for something.

The seven-hour time difference between us and Afghanistan also added to the awkwardness. If he called first thing in the morning for him, we were winding down at home and I was utterly exhausted. Or he often telephoned when I was right in the middle of getting the kids off to school with not much chance of stopping the morning routine. There was hardly ever a "good" time. We just had to make do.

I knew he needed to hear from the kids and from me though. He was lonely, a little down, and missed us. When the novelty and excitement of deployment started to wear off, he faced ten more months of living, sleeping, eating, and exercising in the same compound. He worked six days a week and did catch up on the seventh. The four-day rest-and-recreation pass that he had previously declined was now back on the table. Deployment challenged even his formidable endurance and work ethic, and he was wise enough to recognize it.

Communication issues between Brad and me were legion, of which awkward telephone conversations were but one example. For years, our interactions were stunted affairs, even when face to face. This passage, copied to my quote journal from an advice website, described us:

> Points get missed, subjects get changed, issues get ignored, important details get glossed over. We alluded to matters indirectly when we ought to confront them boldly, thus we created endless spirals of misunderstanding. The cycle of insufficient communication took us to various points of frustration and to experiences of deep disappointment. (Cainer)

Everyday dialogues were an obstacle course of miscues and snafus. Since the beginning of the marriage, the shortcoming had always frustrated me more than him.

"We may not have that 'conversational chemistry' that you yearn for," Brad wrote in a letter to me in 2003, "but I hope you and I can start on a fresh communication slate."

"Conversational chemistry" was a trivial way of expressing this profound problem at the heart of our marriage. We had no ease of communication. Brad being gone so much had masked the seriousness of the malfunction because with our parallel lives—his with the Army elsewhere and mine at home—we kept in touch with businesslike information bits sent via letters and e-mail, thus avoiding potholes.

This wasn't the Mars/Venus thing—that cliché had been done and overdone. It was closer to say he was an Apple Computer and I was a PC. Our operating systems were so incompatible that we couldn't interface without downloading extra software, add-ons, updates, and patches to bridge the gaps, and even then the translations could be unintelligible, the parts impossible to assimilate. "It shouldn't be this hard," I'd complained often.

One of the five marriage counselors we saw observed that we had a **VERY** (and she really did say it in bold face, all caps) pronounced male-female disconnect. Another gave us couples' communication exercises to practice at home, adding as we left her office, "Good luck. You guys need it."

We were the poster couple for the empathizing-systemizing theory. Of the two, I had the empathizing brain—compassionate, good at communicating, able to tune in to people intuitively. Brad's was a systemizing brain, comfortable with things that had a set of rules and followed a logical pattern. In other words, understanding shape-shifting, unpredictable me was like pinning jelly to the wall for him. Frighteningly, this hairline crack had come up at our pre-marriage counseling sessions with the Catholic diocese. A psychologist-trained nun examined the results of our Briggs-Myers Personality Inventories and predicted—quite accurately, as it turned out—our future challenges: "Marna looks out the window and daydreams, imagines, and loses track of time. Brad looks out the window and sees it needs to be washed." These whispers of incompatibility, brushed off as we eagerly planned our wedding, had mushroomed into roadblocks over the years.

I was Wi-Fi in the relationship, connecting dots quickly and grasping nuanced issues effortlessly, especially those involving human nature and relationships. Brad often couldn't follow my conversation. If he synthesized, he came up with the wrong conclusion or missed the point entirely. Worse, because he didn't really believe in my intuitive methods, he routinely dismissed me. After seventeen years of my observations, interpretations, and assessments being proven correct, it hurt that he still ignored me in favor of some dogmatic GPS, even if the pre-loaded maps were outdated and the directions sent us to the bottom of a lake. That was the problem when he navigated by ideals—he missed so much reality.

His behavior fed my gnawing suspicion that he never really listened to me. My voice was the nonsensical gibberish of off-camera adults in Charlie Brown cartoons.

"There's that new coffee roasting shop our neighbor mentioned," I said as we passed a strip mall. Brad didn't respond or look where I pointed. Crickets. Rather than provoke an argument by saying, "Did you hear me?" I stayed silent. Less than half an hour later we were returning on the same road, and he pointed out the store. "Look, there's the coffee roasting place Jim loves," he said excitedly.

"I just said that, Brad. Literally. Fifteen minutes ago."

"I didn't know you were talking to me," he said.

"You're the only other human being in the car. Who else would I be talking to?"

He just grinned as if he'd been caught sneaking extra dessert instead of confirming my worst fear—that he tuned me out.

One time Brad and I were discussing the best way to get into Boston for a Red Sox game. I wanted to drive to an outlying stop and take the subway into Fenway Park.

"Not a good idea," he countered. "The trains stop running before the game ends. We'll be stuck at the ballpark."

"The subways run late."

"The last train is at 8. I checked."

"I'm talking about the subway. We took the subway after the game last time, remember? It was fine."

"I don't want to take the train."

"I'm not talking about the train," I shrieked. "The subway! Not the train!"

He stared at me for a long time before I saw his light bulb moment. "Oh, you're talking about the subway, not the train."

"Yes, I've been talking about the subway the whole time."

These thickets were pure torture for me. I knew he had missed the point, but we couldn't come to an understanding because he didn't realize he'd taken a wrong turn. Sometimes things balled up so badly that I had to insist, "Forget what you think you know. Go back to our last known point and start over." There were layers upon layers of knots to unravel. We moved in maddening fits and starts, and even straight-forward logistical exchanges required herculean efforts.

I developed a sixth sense for detecting when we had broken contact. It was like hearing dead air between two frequencies when you're tuning an old-fashioned radio. If I didn't get his attention back right away, things quickly disintegrated.

These deficit conditions made everyday matters arduous, and more sophisticated subjects were often out of the question. Brad didn't see it as a problem the way I did because to him, it fell under the innocuous umbrella of "conversational chemistry." After years of annoying talk troubles, I thought he should take measures to ensure they didn't happen or at least happened less frequently. For example, he could pay more attention when I spoke and remind himself, "This was tricky with us. Proceed mindfully." Or repeat back what he'd heard me say in order to ensure he'd processed accurately, the way the marriage counselors coached us: "Marna, I'm hearing you say . . ." And he could stop walking out of the room when I spoke, a practice I'd also seen his father do with his mother.

His behaviors that sabotaged our communication, such as interrupting, lack of eye contact, and hair-trigger distractibility, were just bad habits, I reasoned, and they could be changed if he wanted. It required only correction and self-discipline. There was little improvement over the years, however, and I interpreted this as an attitude of "What can Marna say that is worthwhile?" If he was interested in what I felt and noticed, he would pay attention, but he didn't, and it broke my heart. My most fundamental human longings—See me, Hear me, Understand me—were going unmet. This wasn't just conversational chemistry—it was a partnership flaw.

With geographical distance between us, our pathways of communication were understandably disrupted and diminished, so I dialed down my expectations. E-mail and snail mail mitigated the micro-annoyances we experienced in person. He missed us, he said often in his letters. I missed us too, but I missed the intense, full-on accord of our early couplehood, when I was more than static to him.

COMMUNICATION CHECKLIST

Setting up parameters and expectations for communication during deployment is one of the most important conversations you can have. At a minimum, this should include how to get in touch with your service member quickly if necessary. For most units, this will be to contact the family readiness group leader or the rear detachment commander. We didn't have a unit because Brad was an individual augmentee, so I got the long-distance phone number with country code to reach him at work.

1. Decide how you feel about the different modes of communication—e-mail, letters, telephone, Skype, or Facetime—and discuss what's available given the location and tactical circumstances.
2. Do regular e-mails take the place of letters and cards? Our preferences were everyday emails for the immediacy and longer letters once a week.
3. How often do you need to communicate to feel connected? It may be different for each person.
4. If telephone calls are an option, try to establish a fairly consistent time that works for both of you.
5. Decide if you want to try video calls. Our decision was not to do that because the visual component made it too hard on the kids, but you know your family best.
6. Keep a notebook by the phone and jot down topics you need/want to discuss. Take notes as you talk so you can bring up important subjects later in e-mails or letters.
7. Keep the Dad box going. Fill it with care items and mail it regularly. Keep blank customs paperwork in your house so you don't have to do it at the post office.
8. Have patience with the time lag in international calls. Try traditional radio protocol if it gets too frustrating.
9. Send pictures and videos. Brad especially liked the videos we made.
10. Set up a schedule for the children to write, even if it's to add a few lines to an e-mail or to write a message in the spiral notebook like we did.

11. The technique of the one-word answer "Noted" comes in handy for e-mails. If one has just unloaded heavy stuff but the other doesn't have time to answer, he or she responds "Noted," which is code for "I'll get back to you but I can't write now."

12. Consider sending each other a love letter once a week to stay close.

13. Get a second clock in the kitchen and set it to the time in Iraq, Afghanistan, Germany, or wherever your service member is. This will help you feel connected and keep you from having to calculate the time difference.

5

HOW DEPLOYMENT AFFECTS A FAMILY

Loneliness was setting in. I missed the built-in social life of marriage. If I felt like watching a movie, I could turn to Brad and say, "Hey let's go see that new James Bond flick tonight," and off we'd go, now that the kids were old enough to stay by themselves. Without a spouse in the same country, I had to call three, four, or five different people to round up someone who was available and interested. Sometimes I gave up after the third "no." Other times, if I were desperate enough, I went by myself, feeding from a tub of greasy popcorn in the back row and sinking low in my seat.

People socialized two by two, I noticed. Normal couple gatherings fell by the wayside as I became increasingly invisible to our circle. Was it because, as an acquaintance posed, people suspected the motives of a husbandless woman, as if I were on the prowl for a placeholder while Brad was gone? I didn't know, but regular inclusion became rare. In December I heard of a Christmas cocktail party that many of my friends attended, but I wasn't invited. I saw them drive by, the wives dolled up in chandelier earrings and faux fur jackets, as I opened a can of tuna for dinner.

By nature, I was introverted and recharged by being alone—to a point. Too much solitude had a way of pushing me off the edge into isolation, and then I couldn't remember the last time I had an adult conversation. When Brad deployed with a battalion, other unit wives in the same boat were always up for hanging out together. This time, with

Brad an individual augmentee and us in a civilian community, I didn't have those options.

Socializing had to become more intentional and planned. Brad advised me in an e-mail, "Don't wait for people to call you. Set something up yourself."

I knew I couldn't entertain guests on my own—it was too much work. The house had to be cleaned and presentable, dishes and glassware organized, a menu planned and prepped. Normally if Brad were here, he'd grill the shish kabobs, bartend, pour coffee, tend to guests, and help me clean up afterward. Without that extra hand, I couldn't imagine doing it myself, certainly not when my energy and enthusiasm were already flagging. Having company for dinner was not realistic.

Instead I could reach out in other ways. I wrote these instructions in my weekly planner as a reminder: "Call a friend. Write a friend. Go out with a friend." Right next to that, I kept a running list of people I wanted to check with, that is, "the usual suspects," and even put a smiley face next to their names if I made contact. The ways I managed it varied from a chatty phone call to an invitation for a walk on the bike path or a Pilates class at the YMCA. On other occasions I scheduled an activity like kayaking, a bike ride, lunch, or a movie. Hustling up my own social life was a new challenge for me, but it kept me from imploding.

As if on cue, the universe acknowledged my intentions. A friend e-mailed me—they were going to happy hour after work on Friday. Did I want to join them? Yes, I did. I joked and laughed with Ellie as I, dressed for socializing and wearing makeup for the first time in weeks, left for the restaurant. That evening, I came across a half-finished e-mail Ellie had written to her Dad, and this line caught my eye: "Mom is kind of crabby, but she's happy when she goes out with her friends."

Vacations took on a different cast during deployment. Brad's idea of vacation was puttering around the garage all week, but if I dreamed up a trip, took care of the details, and shoved him in the fully packed car, he'd go and actually enjoy himself once we got there. In spite of his reluctance to spend money, he was Mr. Vacation. He reconnected with the kids, moment to moment, which he couldn't do during the work week. With him on Dad duty, and Ellie and Joe relishing attention from their father, I got a chance to take a break. We swapped roles. They got adventure days and I decompressed, a perfect getaway for all.

When Brad was gone, vacations were all me. No second parent to pick up the slack and no one to run interference. That's why, at the end of the summer, I felt justified in splurging on a long weekend at a small family resort on Cape Cod, where we'd had a wonderful visit several years earlier. We stayed in a cute cottage right near the water. There was also a pool, volleyball, bocce ball, kayaking, and bicycling close at hand. Ellie and Joe found entertainment everywhere on the property and I relaxed by the pool with a book, or we went to the beach together. For breakfast and dinner, we wandered over to the dining room at the inn, and for lunch we ate cheeseburgers at the pool snack shack.

In spite of the amenities, Ellie and Joe missed the intensity of that usual time with their father. Indeed, I think many of their vivid childhood memories with him took place during vacations because that's when he was most present and involved. This time, I sensed a certain mournfulness in Ellie and Joe, but whether it was because Labor Day weekend represented the official end of summer or because the deployment was gnawing at them emotionally, I couldn't tell.

The absence of a second parent expressed itself especially strongly on two days of the year—both in May. I had to drive Joe to the florist because he wanted to buy a Mother's Day gift for me. Right before I detoured into the adjacent greenhouse, I slid him a twenty dollar bill for expenses and then disappeared to find annuals for the window boxes. When he gave me the all clear signal, I showed at the cash register with my flats of purple petunias, while Joe secretively stuffed bags in the back of the car. "Your son is darling," said the cashier, a woman about ten years older than I am. "So sweet. Such a nice boy."

Ever since Joe was little, he's had this effect on people with his natural warmth, empathy, and personality. "He's such a blessing," I said. "His sister too." At these words, the lady shifted from complimentary to misty-eyed. "I'm a little sensitive," she admitted. "I don't have children of my own." It must be hard to work in a flower shop around Mother's Day if that were the case, I thought, silently blessing the woman for tuning my appreciation of my own son.

A week later, my birthday was just another passing day—no coffee in bed or special treatment. I guess Ellie and Joe thought they covered that on Mother's Day. Ellie wanted to go to the high school for a meeting, so I let her drive us there, then I went to the beach for a walk and picked her up on the way home. I exercised my birthday prerogative and directed Ellie and Joe to do a little yard work for me in the afternoon. Joe and I dug up the landscape island while Ellie sanded the peeling paint off the doorjamb of the garage with the palm sander. After a while I took over and she hacked at the sod. When I looked over, she and her brother had staged batting practice in the backyard with hunks of sod and a shovel, clods of dirt spraying everywhere. The two of them made a creative escape out of just about anything.

I asked the kids to put their heads together and come up with something for us to do to celebrate my birthday. "I'll drive. I'll pay for it. Just come up with it," I said, because I was tired of being the chief of entertainment and activities. We could have gone on a hike or a bike ride or another fun thing, but they didn't put any thought into it, and their indifference hurt. There wasn't even a consideration for dinner— like, "Hey mom, take a break because we're cooking your favorite!" At that point, I got a little petulant about someone, anyone besides me, deciding. We ended up going to an overpriced restaurant in town. Twenty-four dollars for salmon, and I even ordered dessert because it was my birthday.

Before Brad left, we ran into a family whose father had just returned from Iraq. "Is that a new car?" asked Brad, pointing to the gleaming SUV. "Yeah," grinned the Guardsman. "A lot happened during deployment."

Service members often came home from overseas to find not only new cars, but new pets, new furniture, and in some cases even a new man in the bed.

When I was in the Army, I once helped another lieutenant move out of her condo while her husband (a class-A jerk who totally deserved this) was training in California for a month. He returned to empty closets and a "Dear John" letter. There was no denying these extended absences offered spouses a natural interval to execute an escape plan.

My mischief was more innocuous. Even though family readiness group leaders counseled us to avoid impulse spending, I made major purchases and undertook extensive home improvement projects when Brad was not around to resist. This was how I got my bone china coffee pot, creamer, and sugar bowl, a new dishwasher, and a Toyota Forerunner. At my college graduation, commencement speaker Admiral Grace Hopper declared it was easier to "beg forgiveness than ask permission," and I followed her advice ever since.

Brad had a long history of unceremoniously rejecting my ideas, so I quit bringing them up to him. In his absence, I acted on them. There was less wear and tear if I just waited until he left. He was fatally allergic to house beautification and needed an EpiPen just to go to Lowe's.

He came home from Kosovo to a redecorated master bedroom with terracotta-colored walls, new bedding, matching curtains, accent pillows, lighting, and accessories. "It's our own bed and breakfast!" he declared when he saw it.

After another extended time away, he returned to find a barely recognizable space next to the kitchen because I'd cleared out the boxes of craft supplies and excavated a real dining room for us. The sewing projects were replaced with elegant drapes, artwork, flower arrangements, and a faux finish on the walls.

I had the eye for bringing beauty, light, and color into our environment, but I could never convince him of the worthiness of this endeavor. Hostage to the bachelor aesthetic of secondhand futons and neon beer signs, Brad thought all home improvement was trite and indulgent. If he could forage a few cinder blocks and planks from a back alley, he'd make some fine shelves for our CDs and paperbacks. Anything beyond that bordered on frivolity. This was a guy who slept on the ground and didn't shower for weeks, I remind you.

I used to joke that whenever I started talking do-it-yourself, Brad interrupted: "The answer's 'No,'" he said. "What was the question?"

"What if we build a breakfast bar onto the kitchen counter?" NO. "Pull up this old fencing?" NO. "Put in a flower bed?" NO. "Redesign the mud room so it's more usable?" NO. "Install a storm door." NO.

So I waited patiently until he left and then began my decorating binges. *Trading Spaces* marathons—the television show where the teams each redid a room for less than $1,000—motivated me, but I tried to keep mine under $500. This time was different. Brad came home on mid-tour leave to find a new driveway roped off and curing. He was four figures worth of livid.

The problems with the driveway were well documented, so I couldn't understand his opposition. The earth beneath the concrete had sunken, creating a depression in the drive that was riddled with very large cracks. After a rain, a lake formed, becoming especially precarious in the winter when temperature cycles froze it into a skating rink or an ankle-deep ice floe right where we entered and exited the car.

But the worst part was that the builder (with no training in design) had planted a landscape island in front of the garage door, so clumsily placed that I had to S turn the minivan around it to get in and out of the garage. After a blizzard—and hey, this was the Northeast—banks of shoveled snow made maneuvering nearly impossible.

On top of that, we had a four-bay driveway abutting our tiny cape. There was so much concrete by the side of our house that it looked like a strip mall. Two of the bays weren't usable because of the landscaping island. There was one parking spot at the far end of the garage and the other right off the back stoop. Our home had many positive qualities, but from the driveway, where everybody formed their first impression, it looked severe and industrial. The lack of curb appeal almost dissuaded me from buying the house.

I invited a landscaper and hardscaper over for a consultation, who recommended we remove the old driveway and landscape island and replace it with space enough for two cars directly in front of the garage. In the process, we could elevate the drive three-quarters of an inch and level it, which would keep the runoff in the street where it belonged.

Mrs. Hippy's hysterical and unsolicited advice upon hearing of my tentative plans was only for the flowering dogwood tree in the island. "You can't rip it out," she protested. Leaving aside for a moment that I could, in fact, rip it out if I wanted because it was my property, and no, I didn't have to offer her first right of refusal, I was personally attached to the lush dogwood and so asked the tree guy if we could relocate it. This led to a predictable phase of home improvement affectionately known as "Mission Creep."

"Sure, we can move it, but that has to go," he pointed to a towering white pine in our postage stamp front yard. When this patch of land had been farm acreage with a rambling house, goats, sheep, and surrounding fields, the tree fit nicely, but next to a modest home built on a plot with narrow street frontage, it looked disproportionate. Besides dripping gutter-clogging pine needles every day, the huge tree shaded the roof, rotting the shingles with constant dampness and lichen buildup.

The lower limbs had been sawed off by previous owners to protect the house and adjacent power lines. From a distance, I could see how misshapen the overall effect was. The arborist told me if the house weren't blocking the wind, the remaining boughs would act as a sail and lift the tree out of the earth, a notion that didn't exactly encourage a peaceful night's sleep.

As if I didn't need more convincing, the tree's root system so close to the house presented a hazard to our foundation, in addition to heaving up the ground around the trunk and preventing grass in that quadrant of the yard.

"I'll call the tree service tomorrow," I said.

The crew of six arrived with chainsaws and a lift and, in a flurry of activity, pared off branches and divided the trunk into six-foot sections. When Ellie returned from school, the pine was laying in pieces in the front yard. "You didn't let me say goodbye," she whined as she scampered over the logs, hugging the bark before peeling her ruined shirt away from the evil pine sap. Joe counted forty-eight rings in the stump. Mrs. Hippy stopped by to register her discontent. "You knew how I felt about trees," she huffed. The good thing about trees, I thought—they grew back. Once the logs were hauled off, the team eased the dogwood to its new location in the front yard, where it flourished.

The landscaper then pulled up with a Bobcat, a dump truck, and an earthmover and ripped out the old driveway. The area was quickly cleared, leveled, and a gorgeous new driveway was poured. This one was perfectly placed in front of the garage with space for two cars and extra room to maneuver bikes, a lawnmower, or a wheelbarrow. "It looks normal now," remarked one of the workers. The improvement was a far cry from the hideous eyesore it had once been.

The side of our house looked so good that I invited the landscaper to lay a brick patio next to the back door and a matching walkway in the front. When he finished, he filled in the privet edge between us and the bike path with rhododendron and cedar and planted arborvitae and perennials by the new patio. It took him three hours to do it, something that would have taken me three days of backbreaking labor and numerous trips to the nursery. Strangers walking by now complimented me on the house as I worked in the yard. Even the water meter reader said, "The place sure looks nice. It just needed you."

My domicile had taken on a personality, wrapping its warm and comforting arms around me every time I came home. One of the deepest drives in a woman was the nesting instinct—making a haven for her brood—and I strongly identified with my role as hearth keeper. Brad didn't understand the toll on me when I couldn't express this. All those years living in cramped, cookie-cutter quarters built by the lowest bidder and randomly assigned to us, I existed in a state of suspended animation because we weren't there long enough to do anything with the space. It was finally time to take chances, and sure, it cost money, but that was the price for the privilege of home ownership.

Brad wasn't happy with the expense. First of all, because it involved concrete, we were talking, as my mother said, "real money."

Second, I didn't ask for permission from him. By the time he found out, it was a done deal, which was my plan exactly. I felt liberated to do the improvements while he was gone. Let the groveling for forgiveness begin.

That was our dynamic and Brad helped create it. I would have loved for him to say, "Marna wants a new driveway. This one is inefficient, dangerous, inconvenient, and downright ugly. I've come to trust her judgment. Let's get some estimates and move forward." Instead he gave me a knee-jerk dismissal: "The water drains after a day or two. Get over it."

I tried to tell him many times that when I asked for something, I really wanted it. I'd vetted my requests thoroughly for practicality and soundness as well as importance to me and rejected many of them in the process. When I finally spoke up, I presented only my top choices, which he then tossed to the scrap heap.

"I don't know why he doesn't listen to me," I confided to my mother. She sensed my pain over this, just as any dissonant family culture was immediately obvious to an outsider. I was a smart woman. Time after time my interpretation and analysis had turned out to be correct, yet I never got any street cred from Brad. It was a zero-sum game with him.

We weren't really arguing about the damn driveway. The disagreement was about something graver—the unhealthy dynamics of being repeatedly dismissed and overlooked by my partner. When Brad was gone, I became the sole decision maker, which simplified matters greatly for me and eliminated having to negotiate with him. My wishes, hopes, and opinions finally had a chance, and I took full advantage. It was sort of like an inmate uprising while the guards slept.

"I'm sorry I didn't ask you," I said with staged contrition because there was nothing he could do about it now. "Just for kicks, tell me your answer if I'd asked."

"No."

I rested my case.

I picked up Joe's collage poster, his response to a school assignment to make a presentation about his family. Next to colorful magazine pictures of baseball players, Army guys, and maps of all the states he'd lived in, there was a family photo. "Sunday is family day at our house," the caption read. "That usually means we have to take a boring walk at some boring nature preserve."

No doubt he was still annoyed over my insistence on family day, a newly implemented time of togetherness on Sundays. He had been invited to play putt-putt with a friend, but I told him no because Sundays were family day and we were taking a field trip, the first one in what I hoped would be a long tradition. He sullenly joined us, but whenever we drove past Adventure Land Golf after that, he grumbled, "I could have gone there but you cheated me."

Joe enjoyed our family outings the most once we actually got to our destination, though he whined, "Do we really have to do this?" even as I backed out of the driveway

Yes, we did. This was my hostile takeover of my children. I was claiming them back from the GameBoy, X-Box, television, telephone, computer, Internet, MySpace, Instant Messenger, and other digital distractions that flung us with centrifugal force to separate corners of our house.

And let's face it; I was springing myself from domestic haze for a while. I wanted to be away from the endless household preoccupations, but I wanted to do it with Joe and Ellie. In order for us to reconnect in the purest way possible, we had to get out.

Family Day was a reassuring antidote to my second biggest deployment anxiety (the first being harm or injury to Brad). The number two fear was that the center would not hold—that I would become an overwhelmed, depressed, and shut down woman as the months progressed.

A disengaged, demoralized mother led to a free-for-all in the family, with Joe lost to video games and Ellie drifting to her circle of Goth-leaning friends. We'd be estranged from each other, lost as a family unit, with no true north or ballast. Then we'd resemble my childhood home, where we all acted like boarders in the same house, barely acknowledging one another as we brushed past in the hallway, shoveling down our meals while standing in the kitchen, and all of us too apathetic to notice or care.

My habit of choice when I was fatigued, hurt, or lonely was to withdraw and tune out—I recognized this tendency. But I was the only parent around and in order to stay present, I had to recharge regularly.

Quiet Sundays out in nature with my children were the solution. The three of us powered down together. I savored time with them and unburdened myself of the notion that I was taking their childhoods for granted. Meanwhile, invaluable life lessons were reinforced, such as how to hatch a thought, carry on a conversation, pay attention, nurture curiosity, explore, notice, and be grateful.

To quote Joe, the first excursion was indeed to a nature preserve, a national wildlife refuge to be exact. Because this was the small, gorgeous state of Rhode Island, there were plenty of them within a short distance, so we went to the one near our house. We hiked several miles on the dirt paths through the woodlands, shrublands, and fields, all the way to the undeveloped coastal salt pond. Climbing up the observation platform, we took in the spectacular view of the late afternoon sun sparkling on the wind-whipped pond. I grew up a landlocked Midwesterner who never tired of gazing at rivers, lakes, and oceans.

On the way back to the car, Joe suddenly remembered that he'd been to this park before and was sure they'd stopped at a geocaching site nearby. We hunted around until we found it in a plastic jar stashed under a bench. He excitedly read the log to us, pointing out where he and his friend wrote their entry the year before.

We stopped at our favorite coffee place on the way home for mugs of hot chocolate topped with mounds of whipped cream, which we slurped while watching a few intrepid boaters steer back to the marina.

"We're done now, right?" Joe asked. "Family day is over?" I nodded—reconnection complete, a happy mom once more. And for the record, it wasn't all day, maybe three hours at the most, but I allocated an entire day to keep it sacrosanct. Joe would never admit it, but he enjoyed the time, and so did Ellie. Sharing, memory making, and the lost art of just hanging out all laid down essential wiring, making them feel grounded, balanced, and loved.

Though there was resistance, we more or less hewed to the Sunday-as-family-day plan for the rest of the year. I even heard Joe tell someone on the phone once, "I can't do it on Sunday. It's family day."

Sometimes our expeditions were low key and spontaneous, like the time I was too tired to drive anywhere, so we walked to the library to drop off a DVD. It was closed but we sat on the bench out front for a while and visited. Then we crossed the street to the playground, settled into swings, and lost ourselves in the rhythms of that classic childhood pastime. Ellie scrambled to the top of the swing set and perched there like a vulture. She's always been a monkey like that, even when she was a little girl. We have so many pictures of her climbing trees. Then Joe had to join her, so they looked like a pair of vultures surveying road kill. On the way downtown, we passed a garage sale and Ellie found a backpack for school. There were two there, and we discussed which one was of higher quality. "This one is made of much sturdier material than the other. And look at the seams—double stitched. That one is already fraying," I said. We bought her the better one and she skipped off happily with it hanging off her shoulder.

We went to the deli/specialty store on Main Street for lunch and wandered the aisles, looking at the artisanal food. "I saw your second-grade teacher in here once," I said to Joe. "She was buying this." I held up a package of ground bison. "What's bison?" asked Ellie. "Buffalo," I said, and they both scrunched up their faces, recollecting, I suspected, the herd that grazed peacefully outside the gates of Fort Leavenworth when we lived in Kansas.

On our walk home, Ellie diverted into the cemetery between the bike path and the river. She showed us her favorite oak tree and the elaborate crypt she and her friend Rachel call "Hedgehog Hill." I pointed out that many of the gravestones, some dating back to the 1700s, had been pushed over. "There's a special place in hell for vandals who did that," I said. "It's so disrespectful."

The bike path was a busy thoroughfare of joggers, walkers, and kids on tricycles. A roving band of four boys on bikes intercepted us—they were on their way to see the twins—and Joe peeled off with them. A little while later all seven of them showed up at our house to shoot baskets. There is nothing so Mayberry wholesome as a group of twelve-year-old boys playing pick-up hoops in the driveway. Before long, they all pushed off on a skateboard adventure. Life on the bike path in our small town offered nonstop, self-propelled recreation.

Much has been said in parenting books (and I've read so many of them!) elevating quality time over quantity time as if they were mutually exclusive. Quantity time may seem prosaic and inconsequential, but anytime you're fully present, it's quality time. That's how I felt at the end of this day. Just by showing up for it, we made it luminous.

I was at Ellie's high school state track meet, where as a sophomore she had qualified for the shot put finals. Because she'd just taken up the sport the previous year, it was indeed an accomplishment. The June weather was sunny and pleasant, and like other onlookers, I peered through the chain link fence at the field events while the races took place on the nearby stadium track. Shot put was a slow-moving, Zen event requiring the athletes to cycle through turns while officials meticulously measured attempts. Waiting gave me a chance to reflect on all the times I'd sat in bleachers and theater seats taking in the milestone events of our children's lives by myself. The litany floated through my memory unbidden on this summery day as I waited for my daughter to step into the circle, a time—like so many others—when I longed for my husband to be next to me, gripping my hand and offering reassuring squeezes. There were so many unshared moments.

Brad missed the high school talent show when the curtain opened to a vignette of Ellie and two friends wearing existential black outfits and sunglasses. Grimly, deadpan, they began reciting "Fuzzy Wuzzy was a bear / Fuzzy Wuzzy had no hair / Fuzzy Wuzzy wasn't fuzzy, was he?" to the applause of the audience. He wasn't around to see her last piano recital or the Christmas pageant either.

Earlier in the fall, Ellie and I found our way to seats in the "cafetorium," a multipurpose, tiered room of cafeteria tables that miraculously converted to benches that faced the stage. We came to watch the middle school drama club perform *Cinderella*, with Joe as one of the villagers. He wore the Legolas tunic I'd fashioned for him at Halloween out of a woolen shirt from the thrift shop. I had no idea they were rehearsing such an elaborate production when he stayed after school two afternoons a week. In the spring Ellie and I again sat together on the cafeteria benches, the two of us beaming with pride as Joe played Oberon—the lead character—in Shakespeare's *A Midsummer Night's Dream.* He'd caught the thespian bug, or maybe it was just his social outlet because I noticed all his friends were in the cast. They were swathed in bed sheets embellished with sprigs of greenery as befitted woodland spirits. If only his Dad could see him doing such a fine job, I thought, performing in front of friends, teachers, and parents and carrying off his role with such aplomb.

I poured it on afterward, telling Joe how proud of him I was, how memorizing all those lines was such an accomplishment, a lead in the play—wow!—and he didn't even look nervous! He wanted to go out for ice cream with the crew to celebrate so I slipped him enough money to buy a triple banana split if he wanted. "You were great," I whispered in his ear as he tolerated my hug. By then he was used to getting double shots of compliments from Mom. I was the one who showed up, who marked the occasion, who took pictures, and who captioned them in scrapbooks. I tried and overtried to make up for the missing parent.

When they were younger, Ellie and Joe both received the top recognition in their grade, "The Pride of the Hive," for academic excellence and citizenship. "Hold up your certificates," I directed after the school ceremony, fighting back my tears. "Let's take a picture for Daddy." Brad was in Kosovo at the time and he wasn't able to witness this precious moment, but we told him about it later.

During back-to-school nights in the fall, I sprinted solo through the unfamiliar hallways, navigating blindly to my next classroom, and I always asked teachers for an extra set of handouts to put in Brad's care package. I scribbled notes in parent/teacher conferences so I could report back to Brad in full during our next telephone call. At Joe's all star baseball games, I recorded the highlights of each inning in our spiral notebook so Brad could enjoy the recap.

Sensitive to Joe's formative pre-adolescence, I attempted to be both nurturing mother and energetic, derring-do father while Brad was gone. One weekend we set off by train to New York City to watch a Yankees game and tour the Empire State Building. I took him skiing in New Hampshire because one shouldn't go through a New England winter without some downhill action (Ellie wasn't interested). He patiently made a few slow runs with me before I cut him loose to tackle the black diamond slopes, "Idiot's Option" being his favorite. He made the best of the trip, but my heart ached because these were memories he should have been having with his father too.

The *coup de gras* occurred while I was watching Joe play rec league basketball not long after our ski trip. My good friend Sue sat with me in the bleachers and mentioned that it was necktie day at the middle school last week but she didn't know how to tie her son's necktie.

"I told him to ask Mr. Reynolds when he got to school," she said. Mr. Reynolds incorporated inspired methods like fantasy football into his math curriculum, which made him a favorite teacher among the seventh-grade boys.

"When he got home I asked him who tied his tie and he said Joe," she said. We exchanged puzzled looks. Joe, my son, who clambered off to school in the mismatched, wrinkled clothes he just picked up off the floor? I didn't know he could even identify a necktie, much less offer instruction on how to wear it. After the game I asked him how he learned to do it.

"You showed me," he said.

I showed him? Talk about unshared moments. A quintessential father-son exchange, a singular rite of passage, like shaving for the first time, didn't happen with Brad but with me. Worse, I couldn't recall tutoring Joe—I just stepped up, fixed it, and forgot about it. I'd become so habituated to filling in for the missing parent that I didn't even think about it anymore. Normalcy was Brad absent from the subtle and significant occasions that made up our days.

This was what growing apart looked like, I thought. The realization settled over me like a stalled front, viscous and oppressive. Circumstances that I thought were just temporary had sneakily robbed my children of years with their father.

Ellie was the sensitive, artistic child I'd fretted over for years, worried that we were damaging her with all this moving around (three schools in three years!). I cringed to recall the times I'd seen her sitting alone at the bus stop, the school assembly, or the playground.

Imagine my surprise when she came home from school in tenth grade and asked if I'd go with her to a program about being a foreign exchange student. The girl who had started over with no friends so many times was now choosing—*choosing*—to be the outsider.

"Well sure honey, I'd be happy to go with you," I said in my chirpiest voice. I wanted my children to feel their aspirations were supported emotionally, financially, or logistically, but as I followed Ellie into the classroom at the high school that evening, a few phrases played in an infinite loop in my head:

This ain't happening. This *definitely* ain't happening. No way, no how.

I'd be a proponent of study abroad in college, but I was dead set against any high school trips to foreign countries alone. For a year? Oh hell no.

Yet I sat down at the table and feigned openmindedness as the representative described her organization. After the carnage of WWI, the American Ambulance Field Service banded together with the common goal of encouraging better relationships among countries in the future. Out of that emerged AFS, an organization dedicated to international study.

Several parents brought their testimonials to the presentation. "Why wouldn't you want to send your teenager away?" posed the handsome, well-dressed father whose son had gone to Germany. "Let someone else worry about enforcing curfews." Admittedly, in my exhausted state, that sounded pretty good.

"We recommend a year program, not a semester," chimed in the equally refined looking mother. "They don't even learn to speak the language until they've been there four months."

With a legal-sized pad of paper in front of me, I formulated my list of questions and concerns. Each time I lobbed one to the panel, they fielded it beautifully. "How do you screen the potential host families?" "What kind of infrastructure is in place if there's an emergency?" Again and again the parents and representative reassured me with their knowledge and professionalism. It was the most thorough example of persuasion I'd ever experienced.

The loop slowly stopped cycling. On the way home, I said to Ellie, "Let's see if we can make this happen." The next day she began filling out the thick packet of application paperwork, writing her letter of intent, and seeking teacher recommendations.

Convincing her father was another matter. He was dead set against it, not because of safety and security concerns, but because she would depart just one month after he returned from Afghanistan.

"I won't get to spend any time with her," he objected. "I haven't seen her all year."

While I understood his position strictly from a rational standpoint, another part of me was outraged. *How dare you?* I silently ranted. *How dare you ask us all to cinch our lives and shrink our horizons because of you? We're not just moons in your orbit. Your career cannot suck all the oxygen out of a room while the rest of us wither and die.*

Perhaps because I had lost touch with so many of my personal aspirations in deference to his career, I was loaded to advocate on Ellie's behalf. In an astonishingly moderate tone, I explained to Brad that junior year was the best time for her to do this. We couldn't wait until senior year so the two of them had a chance to get reacquainted. They would just have to make the most of their month together, and believe me, he wouldn't regret this.

The overseas phone connection between us crackled and hissed. "I'm just not ready to let her go," he admitted.

"Oh, Brad," I said quietly. "She's already left us."

Our spirited girl, who had strained for independence since she was little, went to Argentina for a year, learned Spanish, made lifelong friends, traveled all over South America, and returned to us with her wanderlust in full flower. At her high school graduation, the valedictorian cited Ellie as someone who "does things and goes places most of us only dream about." There was a gap year in Germany and journeys through Europe after high school. We didn't know it then, but post-college she would join the Peace Corps and live in Eastern Europe, where she learned Ukrainian and Russian. I liked to think Ellie's path opened up when her father and I let go, even though we left claw marks as we did it.

Thanks to the largesse of the university president who admired Brad as "a soldier and a scholar" and who supported the ROTC Department, our family was invited to watch all the home basketball games from the VIP suite high atop the arena. During those long New England winters, it was wonderful to have the diversion and excitement of an outing to the game once or twice a week. Tonight I came with Joe and a friend of his who had plowed through the buffet table of shrimp cocktail, chicken tenders, and mini cheesecakes and pillaged the vat of iced soft drinks since arriving. They now sat in the seats happily munching popcorn and watching the game, the picture of boyish camaraderie.

I began talking with the dean of student affairs, a youthful looking, incredibly warm man who used to play pickup basketball with Brad at lunch time. Since Brad left, the dean had called the house once a month to check on the kids and me, always asking if there was anything he could do to help us, and I appreciated being remembered for such a sustained period. He and Brad also exchanged e-mails regularly. Just before Christmas, Brad sent a box from Afghanistan with, among other things, gifts for the dean to thank him for his kindnesses. I wrapped them in red tissue paper, tucked them in a pretty holiday bag, and delivered them to his office at the student union. The dean was so surprised and touched that he opened the gift right then—a brown wool Karakul (the traditional Afghan hat President Hamid Karzai always wore that looked like an upended rowboat) and a soft Keffieyeh neck scarf. He put on the wool cap, draped the scarf around his shoulders with a regal flourish, and declared, "I'm the president of Rhode Island." When nobody bowed, he said, "Okay, maybe just the president of the student union." Again, nothing. Crestfallen, he removed the hat and slunk back to his desk, but his show left the secretary and me in stitches.

Tonight this kind man and I sat together in the plush armchairs of the lounge, apart from the noise of the game. Campus lights twinkled on the hill beyond the picture window. It was the first time I'd seen him since his hilarious pantomime, and there was obviously something on his mind. He said Brad had confided his worries that we were flourishing in his absence and that he had worked himself out of a place in the family.

"I reassured him that you're doing well, but you all miss him terribly," he said. I smiled and nodded agreeably because this was what people wanted to see.

The truth was that I was surprised at how quickly and easily we functioned without him.

No doubt Ellie and Joe felt pangs from time to time, but they were rolling along with their lives, school, friends, sports, and activities, largely because I worked tirelessly to maintain a schedule and sense of consistency. Throughout their lives, their Dad had always departed for short and long periods of time, to the point where one morning Joe looked up and asked, "Where's Dad?"

"Washington State," I said. "Remember we talked about it?"

"When is he coming back?"

"In eight weeks."

"Okay," he said, and went back to absently reading the cereal box.

"You and the kids will just put me up on the shelf and take me down every now and then to check the expiration date," Brad counseled before he left, borrowing the oft-repeated tactic of military families. And he had seemed fine with that advice, but the reality of it bothered him now.

He wanted us to function but not thrive because then he felt superfluous. He wanted to see a tiny bit of emotional angst at his removal from the family, just to know he added something to the operation.

In the basketball arena, the crowds cheered, the buzzer sounded, and music thrummed. I looked at this administrator, whose daily job was to counsel and smooth out problems and who so deeply wanted to accomplish that right now. He took his charge to look after the soldier's family on his watch seriously.

"The kids and I," I said dispassionately, "of course we miss him every day." With my admission, the dean visibly relaxed and we both turned back to the game.

The part I couldn't tell him—couldn't tell anyone—was that I really didn't miss Brad, nor long for him in the wee hours of the morning. Maybe he had worked himself out of a job, at least in my life. Whether he was gone or present, I had the same tepid feelings about him and our marriage.

Not only had I put him on the shelf, I'd moved him to the back of the root cellar, turned out the lights, and locked the door.

Many times in the past seventeen years I'd fantasized about leaving this marriage, just packing up suitcases for me and the kids, loading them in the backseat, and driving off to an undisclosed, out-of-state location. Brad would have been one of those oblivious men who said, "I don't know why she left. We were so happy."

Yet every fantasy of leaving ended with this jarring dose of reality: me as a single working mother waking my two little ones at an ungodly hour from a peaceful sleep, dressing their comatose selves, force-feeding them a granola bar, and shoving them into car seats for the ride to day care. After work, dead tired, I'd pick them up, offering not my nurturing, patient self but a tired, short-tempered, stressed, and hungry one. We'd probably order pizza for dinner and I'd catch up on laundry or bill paying in our little apartment while they watched television. Then we'd do it all again the next day and nothing about that lifestyle appealed.

When we lived in upstate New York, I'd seen the neighbor carting her toddler to the car at 6:45 a.m. while I sipped coffee at my kitchen table. An hour later, my own preschooler shuffled downstairs in footie pajamas and climbed up in my lap for a morning cuddle. That leisurely routine was how we started our day, with him knowing I was here, ready and waiting.

I wanted to be a mom who was around. My own mother did it when we were young, until financial circumstances forced her to work full time as a secretary. Later, a divorce ended family life as we knew it. My father moved three hours away to take a job in another city, and my mother was gone all day.

Often in high school I'd come home in the evening after working on the school paper or playing in a volleyball tournament to find a darkened house and my three younger sisters huddled around the blue light of the television. We didn't know where our mother was or when she'd be home—it could be seven or eleven, or if she were traveling, she didn't come home at all. I realized now how odd the situation was, but at the time it was just how things were at our house.

I'd rummage in the cupboards for something to fix for dinner, which was usually canned hash, Hamburger Helper, macaroni and cheese. Many times there was just a light bulb and a head of brown iceberg lettuce in the refrigerator. Provisions in our house were touch and go. That's why, once I became an adult and managed my own kitchen, I kept the larder well stocked. "Comfort food" to me meant a bounty of fresh fruits and vegetables, butter, milk, eggs, chicken, beef, and cheese—all the pantry staples needed to make delicious, healthy meals from scratch.

These early conditions also explained why I was so attached to the evening vignette of me plying my evening care, roast in the oven, dinner table set, Ellie practicing her piano, and Joe doing his homework at the breakfast bar. To me this was the kind of scenario I had always wanted waiting for me—a clean, well-lighted place.

I couldn't impose the craziness and chaos on them that I'd experienced. To be working and unmarried, with latchkey or day care kids, was to be right back in my mother's shoes. Although during bad times in my marriage I threatened leaving, I still tried the scenario on for size and I couldn't talk myself into it. The profound wish to make a protective, nurturing home for Ellie and Joe was more compelling. Brad was the sole breadwinner and that excused a multitude of sins. It wasn't perfect, but at least I got to be the kind of mother I wanted to be, which was awake, aware, and available.

6

MISHAPS AND MURPHY'S LAW

Military spouses often commiserated about deployment gremlins—those trolls who release their turmoil moments after the service member leaves for an extended period. They sabotage the air conditioner during a heat wave and then break open a vial of stomach flu to cycle through the household.

We've had some noteworthy examples of gremlins in our household. One morning, just as daylight filtered through the shades, Joe, then a preschooler, shuffled into my bedroom crying. "This hurts," he sniffled, pulling up his pajama top to reveal a red spot on his rib cage.

I sat up in bed and scooted closer to get a better look. "Honey," I said, "You have chickenpox."

How in the cornbread hell did such rotten luck happen? Brad had literally just kissed me goodbye in the predawn hours and left for a ten-day field problem. That meant he was out of contact with me (short of a Red Cross message), and I would be under house arrest alone with Joe for the duration of the contagious disease. Fortunately, Ellie had chicken pox years earlier, so I only had to get her on the school bus in the morning; piano lessons and soccer were out of the question. Because of the kindness of my neighbor, who brought over a fresh gallon of milk when we ran out, we had breakfast food in the house.

I called the friend who'd been over for dinner the night before with her daughter. "Head's up," I said, "Joe came down with chicken pox this morning. He was contagious when you were here." Not to worry, she assured me. They'd been through it.

"Of course Brad is in the field so I can't call him or e-mail him," I told her. But with the rapid fire efficiency of the wives' network, my friend mentioned it to her husband, who hadn't left for the field yet, and who then filled Brad in once they saw each other. The battalion commander allowed Brad to call home. I could tell by his super-apologetic tone that he felt terrible he couldn't be there. "I know, I know," I said wearily. By the time Brad got home nearly two weeks later, the sores covering Joe's face and body were scabbed over and healing nicely.

Once Brad packed up his SUV and departed for two months to attend a staff course in Kansas, pausing briefly on his way out of town to call me from a pay phone (again, pre–cell phones). He'd just heard on the radio that a blizzard was headed my way. "They're forecasting at least a foot of snow tomorrow," he said. I shifted our daughter from one hip to another. "Better make sure you have a snow shovel handy," he added. Right. A blizzard. A baby. Brad gone. Of course.

Another time, again while Brad was absent, hurricane-force winds ripped through the area, lifting our shed off the ground and wrapping it around a tree in the backyard. After the storm, I walked around the neighborhood, collecting our soaked belongings in a wheelbarrow and piling them in the laundry room to dry because we had no garage, no carport, and now no shed.

No two stretches of military life were alike, and the Afghanistan deployment offered up its own fresh hell.

The late morning was impossibly overcast and rainy and I was looking forward to a "desk" day at home after dropping my daughter off at school and running errands. On Thursdays, my housekeeper came, so I planned to balance the checkbook, pay bills, make a grocery list, catch up on phone calls, and take care of other administrivia, hopefully finishing early enough for some down time before the kids returned from school. I was on the last leg of my drive home, daydreaming about a cup of freshly brewed coffee, when I saw flashing blue lights in my rear view mirror. A squad car? Sure, I was going five miles per hour above the speed limit, but I was still the slowest vehicle on the road.

I pulled over and reached for my license and registration while the police officer sidled up to my window. "Good morning, ma'am," he said pleasantly. "You're the colonel's wife, aren't you?" I recognized him then. He was a Rhode Island Guardsman who had once deployed to Iraq for a year and had attended several ROTC events at the university. "Yes," I said, smiling brightly, happy to make small talk for a few minutes. This was nothing more than a village social call, I decided.

"Ma'am, the reason I pulled you over is because your registration expired a year ago." A year ago? I fished through documents from the glove compartment hoping that I had just forgotten to apply the decal. No luck. We had never renewed the registration.

"Now normally," the officer said as he easily slipped back into law enforcement persona, "we'd give you a ticket, impound the car, and tow it. But I'll tell you what," he continued glibly, "I'll pretend this traffic stop never happened if you promise to take care of it today."

Feeling very obliging, I assured him I would, so instead of a low-key day at home, I faced the exquisite torture known as the Rhode Island Department of Motor Vehicles. I checked in at home with my housekeeper, wrote her a check because I wouldn't see her for the rest of the day, ate a snack, packed provisions, grabbed a stack of magazines, and headed to the local license branch.

I wondered what the tired municipal building used to be (it had that repurposed look) as I walked in and tore off a ticket, the kind you get at the deli counter, which informed me of at least an hour's stay. Why were these places so dreary? Harsh institutional fluorescent lights illuminated signs penned in black Magic Marker and taped to the wall. This was customer service at its finest: "We DO NOT accept credit cards." "You must show actual Social Security card, not a copy!" and the only redeeming one of the bunch: "Turn off cell phones." Otherwise, I couldn't escape the gum snappers obliviously carrying on their trite, loud, one-way conversations.

"NO registration renewals at counter!" another sign on green copy paper declared. I wasn't going to wait for an hour to be told I couldn't do what I needed to do. I should ask a human. Another sign stopped me: "Do NOT talk to the clerk unless YOUR number is CALLED." I walked out to the hallway and placed a call to the main telephone number hoping to reach someone with a pulse. Instead I waded through countless menu options delivered by a robovoice. Nor did any of the official forms in the racks offer answers. This was before smartphones, but I wished I'd brought my laptop with wireless Internet connection. I scooted to the public library down the street to research my

DMV question on their computer and discovered with renewals two months or more overdue, I had to complete it at the counter. I sped back to the DMV, but they were past my number when I got there. I took another ticket and settled in the dugout bench to read my magazines. Normally I steeled myself that I wouldn't be able to complete my business in one trip, but I thought, maybe, just maybe, I could do it today. When they called my new number after about forty-five minutes, I handed over my paperwork and the clerk looked up our record.

"We'll have to do an all new registration," she said. "Where's Brad? He'll have to sign."

"Deployed," I said. "But I can sign. I have power of attorney."

"Can I see it?"

Well, wouldn't you know? That was one document I forgot to bring. Our cars were registered under Brad's name to take advantage of a tax waiver for military. Several years earlier, I had gotten a speeding ticket and I couldn't even stand before the judge in traffic tribunal because the car wasn't registered in my name. Brad had to be there.

"Fill out this form and bring it back with the power of attorney," the clerk instructed.

"What else do I need to complete this," I asked, "like proof of residency, utility bill, insurance documentation, green card, marriage license, military orders, car title, living will, birth certificate? If there's anything else I might possibly need, can you tell me now?"

The clerk was getting testy with me, and I with her, but I was hoping to uncover some pesky detail that would prevent a fourth visit. Because finishing today wasn't possible, I stuffed all the paperwork back into a folder.

"Guess I'll be back tomorrow," I said, which was how I ended an e-mail to a friend recounting my wasted day.

She immediately replied, "You probably knew this, but the Wakefield DMV is not open tomorrow. You'll have to go to Westerly," a town forty-five minutes south. "Or," she added helpfully, "wait until Monday. At least no ticket and in this town that's a miracle. Thank God for networking."

Every five years or so we hired a professional to do our taxes, just to make sure we were on track with everything and wouldn't be blindsided with a delinquency or worse a credit we failed to take.

This was not one of those years, but it was a special situation and I should have insisted we use an accountant. I'm not sure Brad would have even agreed to it, being a frugal guy. Except it wasn't him doing taxes—it was me.

Brad had been a major positive influence in the arena of personal finances. He faced bills, debts, and checkbook balances head on while I ducked and covered. Money, or more precisely *lack of money*, was a button for me. It was an exaggerated response to my upbringing in a family of very modest means during the recession of the 1970s. The threat of financial ruin—bankruptcy, homelessness, car repossession— was ever present in my formative years, which led to some neurotic attitudes toward money in my adult life.

The first year Brad and I were married, I stashed my W2 in a file box somewhere and forgot about it. It was only January and taxes weren't due until April. What was the hurry?

"Let's do the taxes this weekend," Brad mentioned more than once.

"There's no rush."

After several repetitions of this conversation, my delay tactics exasperated him. "You don't have to wait until the last minute to file your taxes," he lectured. "You can do it the day you get your W2."

This was a revelation. I had always put it off until the last minute and didn't know there was any other way. Looking back at my childhood, I recalled my earliest tax memory was sitting in the car with my mother on April 15. It was dark outside and by all ten watts of interior light, she was doing her taxes. They were due that day and she'd missed the late pickup at the local post office, which meant we drove to the downtown post office for the midnight pickup. The forms weren't even completed, as evidenced by the stacks arranged on the seat, the dashboard, and her lap, where periodically she scribbled in figures after consulting statements and schedules. This was my role model. The only explanation she gave was, "Why should I give the government my money any sooner than I have to?"

Though I remained unconvinced of Brad's early time line, I fetched my W2 from the closet, rather like a small child producing the pilfered bag of marshmallows. With just the two of us—no house, no children, no fancy investments, odd income, or loopholes—Brad filled out the 1040 before noon. We leisurely deposited the return in the mailbox on the way to lunch. After years of sprinting to the post office at midnight, it felt freakish, against nature.

Brad's persistent, intolerant, and impatient tutelage over the years helped desensitize my money panic. Sometimes I had to remind myself to breathe or use a similar self-calming technique when I paid bills, but that was the only vestige.

Now, huddled over a mountain of IRS forms while Brad was gone, I started hyperventilating again. Straightforward tax returns were a thing of the past. With home ownership, we'd started itemizing deductions, and for the first time I was figuring a home office deduction because I'd generated income with my published book. For almost a week I'd taken over the dining room table sorting stacks of receipts, statements, tax schedules, W2s, 1099s, and spreadsheets.

And it was taking up *all my time*.

Even with Turbo Tax on the laptop next to me, progress was maddening. The directions in the IRS booklet were so confusing that I reread them three or four times and still had to repeat steps in my calculations. This continued until about three in the afternoon, a time when I hit my energetic low point. Typically this was when Brad chose to call. Not only was I too distracted and preoccupied to have a proper conversation with him, but he became the downrange target for my pent-up rage against the Internal Revenue Service. I'm sure he finished many of those phone conversations staring in disbelief at the receiver.

I also hit him with e-mail rants:

"What is a 'antc cust roth ira' with AIM Summit?"

"I thought the Aim Summit was a traditional."

"Why was $2,369 transferred out?"

"Taxes are a pain in the ass. I've been working on them for three days straight."

"Yes, honey," Brad replied, "I appreciate the work that goes into doing taxes. . . . I've done the taxes in the recent past." He conveniently overlooked the fact that when he did them, he locked himself in a room while I fended off interruptions and inanities like ball practice, dinner, or shuttling our daughter to art classes.

"It's more difficult because of the office deduction, book income, and business expenses. If it were like last year, I'd be done by now."

That was happening a lot during this deployment. I, in a threadbare state, wrote or yelled something I regretted. Even though I apologized afterward, I worried about the cumulative effect of these outbursts on our relationship.

Not for the first time, I held up to the light a drinking glass I'd just taken from the dishwasher. It was opaque. "This dishwasher doesn't clean as well as it used to," I said, wondering if there was a rinse agent I should try. Within a few days, the grime and crud became unsanitary. Plates and cups finished the wash cycle covered with a scrim of food matter. I poked around the bottom of the dishwasher for a few minutes before deciding this was one for the professionals.

The only appliance repair company I knew of informed me their first appointment was a week from the following Thursday. Did I wish to book it? Yes, I did.

In the meantime, we ate our meals off paper plates and bowls and used plastic cups and disposable flatware. True, we could have hand-washed our dishes, but convenience trumped environmental considerations. After dinner, we walked to the garbage and tossed our plates and cups. I felt mildly irresponsible, but told myself it was only temporary.

After digging around in the depths of our dishwasher, the appliance repairman held up a carousel-shaped part he'd removed. It was coated with something resembling spinach pesto. "Here's your problem," he said. "You don't rinse your dishes before you load them." Not true, I thought, but we don't put clean dishes in the dishwasher to be cleaned either. Why did repair people blame customers for every breakdown? He'd call when the part came in, he said, without offering a time frame, and in the meantime we ate picnic style.

Before the part was installed and our dishwasher became operational again, I enjoyed the easy interval when kitchen cleanup consisted of throwing everything away.

"Hey gang," I said, holding a paper plate aloft, "How about we do it this way for the rest of the year?"

Ellie was horrified. "That creates too much garbage for the earth! It goes right into the landfill," she protested. She'd practiced environmental sustainability ever since preschool, when she scolded me for running the faucet while I brushed my teeth. Now the antithesis of a materialistic teenager, she bought clothes at thrift shops, rode a secondhand bike everywhere, and packed her lunch in reusable containers.

As I wrote the technician a check for an unbudgeted dishwasher repair, I was edgy about bad luck. Things came in threes, as the saying went.

I therefore wasn't surprised when the next day malware hijacked our desktop computer, freezing the operating system. Even an hour on the phone with the remote repair specialist couldn't rescue it. The virus magnanimously offered to perform a self-purging operation if only I entered my credit card number.

"Bring it to the shop," advised the tech guy. His business advertised with the slogan "Dragging you clicking and screaming into the 21st century." He was right about the screaming anyway.

My computer joined a lengthy queue of sad-looking components with service orders taped to them. "Those viruses," the rep said, shaking his head. "They code new ones before we've got the most recent anti-virus installed."

"Instant obsolescence," I grimaced.

"Exactly," he said, and his words echoed in my head when I returned to pick up my computer, knowing it probably wouldn't be long before another bug appeared.

My garage refrigerator, or the beer-erator as we called it, quit. Something inside hummed but it wasn't cooling. I used this refrigerator to hold overflow supplies and bulky items, such as a defrosting Thanksgiving turkey, cases of drinks, or watermelon. The extra freezer space was nice for bags of ice to fill the cooler and half-gallons of ice cream bought on sale.

I had discovered the manager of our local Little League, Mr. Grayson, was an appliance repairman, in addition to being a firefighter by trade, so I called him. A gray-haired, kindly if bedraggled-looking fellow, he came over that morning, tinkered with the back of the unit and after about half an hour held up a badly melted plastic widget. "This here is your starter. It burned itself out trying to start," he said.

"Was that a fire hazard?" I asked.

"Yes ma'am," he nodded. He replaced it with a stock part he kept in the truck. "It's running," he reported.

I wanted to write him a check right then but he said, "Let's see if it cools. If it does, I'll send you a bill." I had a feeling he wouldn't charge me though. He asked how Brad was doing and talked about Joe, who played on his fall ball team. "What a great kid," he said. "He had some super plays and I know he wished his dad could see them." I felt a flicker of sadness for Brad and Joe and all the things they hadn't shared. That's why I watched as many games as I could—to make up for Brad's absence. It wasn't the same as Dad seeing Joe on the ball field, though, and this father of two boys, this coach/firefighter/refrigerator repairman, understood.

"While you're here," I pressed, "can you install this part on my vacuum?"

"I don't do vacuums, lady," he replied grumpily, but he swiped the belt from my hand and fixed it anyway.

A few days later, I arrived home to find Joe in the kitchen. "Everything in the outside fridge is frozen," he announced. "Everything."

"No way. It's on the lowest setting," I said. Grayson fixed the starter and now it wouldn't stop. Gallons of milk and bottles of Gatorade had transformed into bulging, misshapen blocks. An entire cantaloupe was frozen solid. I carried the icy hunk into the kitchen and dumped it in the sink. Grayson wasn't even sure his repair would work. Wait until I told him he'd created a beast.

"Nothing is safe," said Joe.

I came out of my house to leave for my job teaching freshman writing at the local university, loaded my three bags into the minivan, and turned the ignition. Silence. Not a chug or a cough or even a valiant effort on the part of my workhorse family vehicle. It was dead.

Fortunately I had a charger pack that my mom had given me, so I popped the hood and attached the cables (basic automotive maintenance being the skill set of every military wife). I tried to jump the battery several times but the engine wouldn't catch.

The clock ticked inexorably to the start time of my class as I contemplated my next move. Should I call the Writing Department and have someone run over to my classroom and announce class was canceled? I didn't want to do that because the semester was so short and there were too few classes to accomplish what we needed.

I decided to call my across-the-street neighbor, Magda, to see if she could give me a ride to campus, and she was happy to shuttle me to the university five miles away.

On that day, I was returning corrected papers to my students, so I had a shopping bag full of folders, my "mom bag" purse, and a rolling backpack containing three textbooks, lesson plans, and handouts. As an adjunct instructor, I didn't have an office on campus, so I schlepped the tools of my trade from home to work and back. Magda dropped me off in front of my academic building moments before class started. "Thanks. I'll catch the bus home," I said, because our houses were just a block from the bus line. I also had reduced price tickets courtesy of the university's mass transportation initiatives.

I dragged and hoisted my cargo up three flights and skidded breathlessly into the already assembled classroom of students. They were accustomed to seeing me disheveled and frenzied, as I'd told them early on that my husband was deployed to Afghanistan. This was one of those days. "All righty then," I said smoothing the light film of perspiration from my brow. "Let me return your papers."

Without a doubt, in the pantheon of neighbors, we had hit the jackpot with Magda and her family. Warm, kind, and generous, she once gave me a ride to the airport at four o'clock in the morning. Her outreach was boundless, and she was always engaged in kindly enterprises, whether it was looking after the youth pastor's toddler or heading up the covered dish drive for her church's Meals on Wheels ministry. She was a woman of incomparable energy and creativity who could help me pin up the hem of a formal dress, bake a wedding cake for the daughter of a friend, and finish repainting her downstairs half-bath, all in one day. We were neighbors because of her thoughtfulness—she gave us the heads up on the retired couple across the street who wanted to sell their house, and we bought it before it was even on the market.

Magda's husband, Rick, a bespectacled, youthful man with strawberry blond hair, was the always-entertaining back-fence neighbor akin to Wilson on *Tool Time*. Whether I needed the answer to a matter of global import or a niggling domestic repair, he delivered it with devastating wit, usually talking so rapidly I could barely follow along.

Rick rode the bike path each morning for exercise—on a unicycle no less, the better to train for his ride up Mount Washington (6,289 feet). He could be found spear fishing in Narragansett Bay in the evenings, outings that were followed by a supply of fresh swordfish steaks delivered to my back door. Or he would tend his peach and apple orchards or install a zipline in the back yard. He once delighted a group of fifth-grade boys by building a hovercraft that actually hovered.

A master electrician, he owned every do-it-yourself tool known to mankind. Whatever I needed, he could find it in his garage or one of his three outbuildings.

"Rick," I quizzed him one day, "do you have any scaffolding?"

"Yes," he said.

"Forty-foot contractor's ladder?" Yes.

"Replacement gear for a garage door opener?" Check.

"Four or more kayaks?" Check.

"Spare parts for a B52?"

"You'll have to go to Quonset for that," he replied without missing a beat.

He was my go-to guy for the honey-do list, not to fix things—I wouldn't ask that of him—but to give me some context to see if there was an easy solution. My single mother made sure I was fluent in minor household repairs, but I'd also lived many years in government quarters where I just phoned in a work order if there was a problem. Rick was always my first call now.

Like the time the heater wouldn't work so I asked him to recommend a furnace repair company. "Before you do that, go to the top of your basement stairs," he instructed. "Is there a red switch there that looks like a light switch?" There was. "Is it switched 'on' or 'off'?" "Off," I said.

"There's your problem. Flip it to on." The vents rattled as the unit shuddered into operation.

Another week I discovered the outlet in the kitchen wasn't working. If I wanted to heat a bagel, I had to carry the toaster to the dining room and plug it in there. Same with the coffee maker. I cycled the circuit breaker in the basement, but it didn't help.

"Think, think," Rick directed me Socratically. "What do you have in the kitchen besides electricity?"

"Food? Water?"

"Bingo," he said.

It dawned on me what had happened—the same thing that happened with bathroom and outdoor outlets. Moisture had tripped the circuit interrupter. I knew immediately what to do. "I should press the reset button," I said.

"Right-O," he said, and slapped me a high five.

Funny enough, neither outlet in the kitchen had a reset button, which struck me as probably not to code. But scouting around, I found another outlet on the same wall in the breakfast nook. I alternately mashed the test and reset buttons a few times for good measure, then walked back to check the coffee maker. It gurgled to life.

When even Rick, the modern Renaissance man, couldn't resuscitate my car, I summoned the tow truck for the ignominious removal to the repair shop. Mrs. Hippy and her two toddlers arrived just in time to watch the spectacle from the safety of my back deck. The boys "oooed" and "ahhhed" as the huge truck noisily pulled my minivan onto its bed. The sheer scale of the endeavor, not to mention the roar of the engine, the muscular winch, and the flashing red lights, was even better than a fire engine. Internal combustion power never failed to entertain young boys—I remembered that from my son's childhood. They clapped and waved as the truck left at a stately pace with my minivan piggybacked to it. Standing on my wide, empty driveway, I watched the inert automobile leave and wondered how much the repairs were going to cost.

The too smooth and slightly smarmy representative at the Mazda service department soon informed me. "Based on a preliminary diagnostic, it'll be at least $2,500," he said. "Maybe more." Was he kidding? We hadn't even finished paying for this car. Practically fainting, I called Rick, who listened carefully to the symptoms and asked me a few questions.

"I'm not convinced it's serious," he announced, "Let's take it to my mechanic."

The next day Rick drove me to the gleaming dealership where the same tow truck driver met us to claim my car. Vinnie at the service desk, in a snowy white button-down and slicked-back hair, was annoyed I planned to seek a second opinion. "I expected a phone call or some notice," he said curtly. Before he let me take my car, he demanded one hundred dollars to cover a diagnostic fee and a hard start. "That's normal," Rick said quietly, so I wrote a check. With another man present, the service manager was more solicitous and guarded and much less transparent about trying to snowball the little lady with the deployed husband. He remained adamant about using Mazda certified mechanics. "They do the best work," he insisted, as Rick pushed me out the door, pausing briefly to grab a glazed cruller from the snack table.

We pulled up to Fix-It-Rite Auto, a facility I thought had closed long ago, and Rick reassured me, "Sam looks like someone from *Deliverance* but he's a great mechanic." This place honest to goodness looked like Goober Pyle's filling station—bare concrete floors, a vast dead bug population on the windowsills, toppling stacks of dog-eared service manuals, and crumpled burger bags stuffed into empty spaces. There was even a gumball machine in the waiting room. I smelled a mixture of gasoline, oil, cigarette smoke, and stale French fries. "I bet there's a girlie calendar in the bathroom," I thought. Sensing my skepticism, Rick persisted, "No really, this is where we bring all my business trucks."

Sam turned out to be a heavyset guy with a full beard and ropes of graying hair pulled back into a ponytail. His fingers, thickly coated with grease, poked at the keyboard of his equally dirty laptop, and there was something that looked suspiciously like moss growing behind his ears. But he was courtly in a swamp Yankee kind of way as he explained the engine malfunction. All appearances to the contrary, Sam seemed like the kind of guy who read Nietzsche at night and made a mean crème brûlée.

Assured it would be fixed within a few days once the parts arrived, we left the minivan in his capable hands. Rick then drove me in his electrician's van to a strip mall in town, where for an additional $200 I rented a subcompact for the week. The young man at the counter told me his father was also in Afghanistan. "He's in the Corps of Engineers," he said. I asked for his name to tell Brad, but nothing came of it. Even though Afghanistan was a big place, Brad's parents, who lived in Virginia Beach, had sold their couch to a Turkish officer who coincidentally knew the Afghan general working with Brad.

Five days later, I strolled down the hill to Fix-It-Rite Auto, paid Sam considerably less than $2,500, and drove my car home. More importantly, I now had a mechanic I could trust, which, as any woman knows, is like a good beautician—invaluable.

Even though the military gave us extra money each pay period during deployments, the gremlins had wiped us out this month. With the car, computer, and dishwasher repairs, not to mention the cost of a rental car, the bank account was reduced to double digits. I nervously recalculated my figures so I wouldn't bounce a check, even postponing a commissary trip until the first of the month while I pieced together odds and ends from the pantry for our meals of black beans, creamed corn, and egg noodles.

PREPARING FOR MURPHY'S LAW CHECKLIST

Attend the pre-deployment briefing and go over the pre-deployment checklist with a fine-toothed comb. Cross every "t" and dot every "i." There are plenty of checklists on the Internet— MilitaryOneSource.com is a good place to start. Make sure you complete the steps, which at a minimum should include:

1. Update wills, power of attorney, and special power of attorney.
2. Locate these documents and keep them in a safe place: passports, birth certificates (certified copies), marriage certificate, car title, and insurance policies.
3. Ensure no military ID cards will expire during the deployment.
4. Confirm DEERs is up to date.
5. Locate spare car keys, house keys, and automatic garage door openers.
6. Complete a list of all the monthly bills and the checking, savings, and investment accounts you have and their usernames, passwords, and PINs.
7. Make sure the life insurance paperwork is up to date and confirm the beneficiaries. You don't want the ex-wife to be the beneficiary. We've all heard the horror stories.
8. Where are the spare checkbooks?
9. Record credit/debit card numbers and keep them in a safe place. Make sure you have the bank phone numbers to report lost/stolen cards.
10. Inventory the contents of your wallet and make a photocopy for your files. In the event your wallet is lost, you'll know what to replace.

11. Make a card with this information and put it in the glove compartment of your car with the registration: "I am the spouse of a deployed service member. If anything happens to me, please notify these people (unit key leader or rear detachment commander and telephone numbers)."
12. If you are an individual augmentee, assemble a team. I asked three friends who were strong, organized, experienced, dependable, and close by to be on my "Comfort Team" if anything happened. I knew they would step in on a moment's notice and handle logistics, airport runs, call screening, and anything else.
13. Discuss funeral wishes and burial plans. A friend of mine recommends you also inform parents of your wishes ahead of time.
14. Make a list of any and all important phone numbers.

And here are some from my own experience:

1. Ensure that the car registration is up to date and in the glove compartment and the new decal is actually applied to the license plate.
2. Do you have a car mechanic you know and trust? Cultivate one before your automobile quits.
3. Make sure you have roadside assistance service.
4. How about an appliance repairperson?
5. Is the heating/air conditioning unit on your house serviced? Do preventive maintenance beforehand.
6. Get the name and number of a recommended plumber and electrician.
7. I highly recommend a go-to person, like my neighbor Rick, who will be your first call in the event of mishaps. He or she can give you information and context that may prevent a service call, for example, "Try cycling the on/off switch a few times."
8. With taxes, consider getting them done professionally or filing an extension and waiting until mid-tour leave to do them together.

7

DEATH OF A FAMILY MEMBER

Bad things come in clusters, and this last one was a doozy.

The answering machine light was blinking when I got home so I hit "Play." The message was from Linda, a neighbor in the subdivision where we'd rented for two years.

"Marna, the Nelson girl was in a car accident last night. I wanted to make sure you knew since you're friends with the family."

I quickly did a Google search.

The Nelsons were players in our "small world" story. When we moved into the duplex, we discovered that Mr. Nelson, down the street, was the brother of Brad's former company commander in Georgia. We now lived in Rhode Island, and the Nelson family was originally from Maine. Go figure.

We became friends with this branch of the Nelsons, often running into them at the nearby lake during the summer. The daughter, Amanda, was then a high school senior but hung out with her mother on the rafts, the two of them splashing around like fellow campers. I thought if my daughter grew up to be like this one—happy, decent, respectful, of good character, and with a passion for some excellence—I'd be a proud parent. Amanda was involved in church mission work and various literacy outreaches. As she laughed and played in the sun, I admired her blonde hair and beautiful features. Every mom wanted her daughter to walk out of the house looking so wholesome and natural.

"Amanda Nelson was pronounced dead at the scene after she lost control of the car she was driving and struck a guardrail in the median after the car rolled over several times," the state police reported.

I felt hollowed out. This was a parent's worst fear—a sudden, violent loss, the life of your nearest and dearest extinguished without warning. Their tragedy was also ours—Amanda was a member of our community, both the geographic one and the emotional one. Her aunt and uncle had been at our wedding seventeen years earlier.

Cici and Bob, also from the old neighborhood, invited me to attend the wake with them. My husband was deployed and their respective spouses were working, so the three of us rode to the funeral home together, the atmosphere between us muted and forlorn. Bob was the athletic alpha male of the neighborhood, leader of the Sunday running club and coach of many youth sports. Cici was the mother of three boys. There would be no coffin at the wake tonight; a memorial service was scheduled in two weeks. When we arrived at the funeral home, mourners stood in a line that snaked around the parking lot. I saw many of Amanda's friends from high school and church and caught sight of the lieutenant governor waiting to pay his respects, a sign of this young woman's remarkable sphere of influence.

We couldn't stop crying as we waited. Every new batch of photograph tributes, lovingly arranged on trifold cardboard displays and placed around the funeral home, reduced us to puddles. Amanda's mother reached up to wipe the tears from my eyes when we were finally face to face in the receiving line. Even in the midst of their sorrow, the family—mother, father, brother, grandmother, boyfriend—comforted mourners for hours.

I found our longtime friends, Tom and Lisa, in the back of the hall. Seventeen years earlier, Tom had kidnapped Brad from our rehearsal dinner for bachelor night antics with the other officers. A captain back then, Tom now wore general's rank, and I'd even seen him on C-SPAN from time to time. Like most military friends with whom we had forged close bonds, the years and distance dissolved when we were together again. This was no different, except the circumstances were unspeakably sad. "Some things are beyond comprehension," Tom said quietly, as we embraced and cried together for a long time.

Cici, Bob, and I walked arm in arm back to the truck, and I was thankful for their company. "Best to do this as a team," Bob agreed.

Anger and agitation were his coping mechanisms. I'd heard him mutter "It's just not right" several times that evening. Cici was actually trembling as I led her through the parking lot.

"I'm not buying any flowers," Bob announced. "I'll send money to her mission work."

Sorrow was the great solvent, I realized, as we opened our hearts to one another on the drive home. For once our conversation transcended the superficial talking points of carpools and baseball rosters and moved into deep reflections about our feeble, imperfect, grasping responses when life threw curveballs.

The next day I stayed in bed, sleeping off layers of fatigue, blowing my nose, sneezing, and nursing a sore throat, not the first time grief had exacted a physical toll on me. I never even changed out of my pajamas. It was a good thing neither kid needed a ride anywhere because I emerged from my room once, dazed and bed-headed, only to traipse back in immediately.

Unfortunately, this was when Brad chose to call from Afghanistan, and I attempted to describe, in my delirious, decongestant-addled state, the events of the previous night. Through tears, I strung together phrases like "so sad," "heartbreaking," and "funeral home was packed."

"Was it open or closed?" Brad interrupted.

"What?"

"The casket. Was it open or closed?" he repeated.

I was speechless. For years I'd been schooling Brad on how to engage emotionally with me during important discussions. This was one of those times when I expected a response such as "How awful. I wish I could have been there for you." Instead he hit me with a data question, something I'd begged him to stop doing in the interest of meaningful communication.

What followed then was a sitcom-worthy moment when the wife storms out of the room, leaving her confused husband behind whimpering, "What? What did I say?" Ours took the form of me silently handing the phone to Ellie and walking away. I was too tired and miserable to make it a teachable moment.

Several weeks later, my son found me at the dining room table reading the day's mail. By then the tide had come back in—pay was deposited, our car and refrigerator hummed along, the dishwasher produced sparkling glassware, and rogue computer bugs stayed at bay. Yet tears rolled down my cheeks. I had just read the Christmas letter from Amanda's family, which this year was a loving eulogy to her.

"I don't know how I'd survive if anything happened to you or Ellie," I said.

"Don't think about that, Mom," said Joe, instinctively hugging me. All the hassles of the past month were just temporary setbacks, pale in comparison to the loss of a daughter in the bloom of her life.

My gaze drifted back to the letter in my hand and fixed on the last lines. *So many dreams as we struggle for what is, what was, and what will never be this side of heaven. Praising His name.*

It was shaping up to be a year of losses, each one knocking me against the ropes in its own inimitable way. Even worse, I was dealing with all this grief by myself. "Shared sorrow is half a sorrow," the Swedish proverb goes, but I had no one around to help shoulder the burden. If our conversation after the Nelson girl died was any indication, talking to Brad on a lagging, static-filled international phone connection was no comfort.

First I had to deal with the drownings of the three students, including my former student, all of whom were presumed dead after they'd been missing several days. Eventually over the next two months, each body was recovered in separate incidents by commercial fishermen trawling the waters of the Narragansett Bay. These incidents were dutifully recorded in a "just-the-facts" tone that belied the anguish of family members and others in this small community.

> The state medical examiner's office has identified the body found floating off Point Judith this morning as Daniel Donahue, 20, of Glocester, one of three University of Rhode Island students believed to have drowned last month. The two other students, Geoffrey M. Wilkes, 18, of Glocester, and Fandia M. Sod Shloul, 21, of Pawtucket, have not been seen since 2:30 a.m. on March 13 when they took a small boat into the foggy, near-freezing waters after attending a small party in the Bonnet Shores area of Narragansett. (Rhode Island Department of Environmental Management Press Release, April 26, 2006)

I hadn't been able to shake the blue mood clinging to me since the search-and-recovery efforts ended. Noticing the funeral announcement of my student in the newspaper and remembering what solace a service was to the mourners after one of Brad's West Point classmates was killed, I decided to attend.

"I'm going to mass today," I announced in the kitchen that morning. Joe, surveying the contents of the refrigerator, peered over the door with a puzzled expression. Ellie paused mid-bite, uncertain if she had heard correctly. Yes, your father was six thousand miles away and I was actually going to mass by myself. I knew it made no sense. I'm Protestant. Their father is a Catholic who browbeat them to mass each Sunday when he was around. On rare occasions, we attended as a family, but in recent years I'd declined regular attendance.

"I still feel so bad about my student's death," I said. "I'm going to his funeral to help me get over it."

We lived in southern Rhode Island and the service was in western Rhode Island, a region of the state with its own microclimate, which I forgot about until I neared my exit. I'd dressed for mild weather when I left the house, but clear skies had given way to overcast ones and chilly drizzle. Without a raincoat or even a sweater, I'd have to make a dash from the parking lot to the church. But what was all this traffic? I didn't recall a shopping center around here. It soon became obvious that cars were lined bumper to bumper from the highway exit down the main street of the town, all inching toward the same service. I hadn't planned for the delay or the crowd, so by the time I finally arrived at the funeral, there were no parking spaces left. I found a spot down the block and trotted back to the modest red brick church, which by now offered standing room only judging by my quick glance through the open door. An outpouring of Rhode Islanders like me had come to say goodbye.

As I stood outside trying to decide if I should stay, I noticed some overflow mourners stationed beneath the church window. I also found a spot under a propped-open pane, where, shivering and wiping away tears, I caught strains of organ music and phrases from the liturgy. I heard one of Dan's brothers say, "We didn't get a chance to say goodbye." They played their guitars and sang one of his favorite songs. Then it was time for the Eucharist. Would they remember those of us outside, I wondered? Some time later, an older gentleman descended the steps holding a tray out questioningly, as if to say "Anybody? Anybody?" I accepted the wafer. "Amen," I prayed as I put the host in my mouth, grateful for even this sidewalk Communion. Although I never converted to Catholicism, the sacraments ushered me through the major events of life and death, and their rituals offered great consolation.

A bagpipe player in the churchyard began the elegiac strains of "Amazing Grace," and its ancient, penetrating skirl threaded through the departing crowd. "Death is the end of all," Thornton Wilder wrote in a novel set on the same bay where the students had drowned. "Death accepted, death united with life in the chain of being from the primal sea to the ultimate cold."

Still grieving, I drove home in the light rain, but an infinite divine order beyond my understanding had been reaffirmed.

Ellie, my little girl, my first baby, was turning sixteen. A college friend had described her daughter's pink-and-brown-themed Sweet Sixteen at their Northern Virginia country club, and I wanted Ellie's to be special in its own way. I offered several suggestions for how we could observe this rite of passage: dinner at a restaurant of her choice, a group to tea in Newport, or how about catching a classic movie at the revival house theater? All met with rejection. She wanted a big pot of homemade vegetable soup made with carrots, celery, tomatoes, parsnips, and potatoes (she's been a vegetarian since middle school), crusty bread, fruit salad with lots of pomegranate seeds, and lemon cupcakes with cream cheese frosting for dessert. She wanted to invite five of her girlfriends over for dinner and watch a video afterward. "Casual, casual," she kept saying.

On the appointed evening, peasant broth simmering on the stove, sweets arranged on the dessert tray, I spread out my fine brocade tablecloth and reached for the good china, but she stopped me.

"No, no, no! That looks too fancy. This is just a sit around and eat kind of thing." Okay, I shrugged, not unhappily. She knew her mind. My role began with supplying provisions and ended with baking cupcakes. Then I was banished during the soiree. I sat on my bed correcting student papers while the voices of high school girls drifted upstairs. Despite the closed door, two girls talked so loudly that I heard almost everything. Eventually I tiptoed over and opened my bedroom door so I could eavesdrop more effectively. Like feigning invisibility while driving a carpool of twelve-year-old boys, it was the time-honored way of learning more about one's teens and tweens.

Ellie's friends were so much more substantial and lively than I remember being at that age, and they really seemed to care for each other. Their conversations, while not overly weighty, were about more than boys, makeup, or gossip, and zigzagged at lightning speed from topic to topic. I strained to hear, soaking up every minute of it.

"Don't you hate it when you're in the car singing and doing the mom bop and someone's been watching you the whole time?"

"What were your favorite books when you were a kid?" "Babar." "The Madeline books." "All the Berenstain Bear books."

"My dad knew the winner of *Survivor*. He was his teacher."

"Guys are high demand. They get bored and need to be entertained. They can't just sit here and talk like this for hours. Talking with your girlfriends is a very special thing, I say."

Late in the night they trooped down to the basement television room to watch *V for Vendetta*. Normally I would have said no, but because this was her birthday, I let them start at 11 p.m. "Come get me when it's time to drive them home," I said and went back to reading, but before long the novel dropped onto my chest and I dozed fitfully with the lamp blazing next to me. At 1 a.m., not the promised 12:30, Ellie roused me to give the three remaining girls a ride home.

We didn't have far to go—everything was close in our New England village—but it was twenty minutes to the other side of town, and in the late mid-winter night, the velvety black seemed especially foreboding. I wasn't accustomed to being out at that hour. We all piled in the minivan and I dropped them off, one by one, at their front doors. Once Ellie's friends were safely returned, we turned back to our place, taking a slightly different route because I thought it was quicker.

I had second thoughts when we rounded a bend and came upon a riot of blue police lights. Was the road blocked? Would we even be able to get through? In semi-rural Rhode Island, some roads were like country lanes—narrow with dense wood lines creeping right up to the easements and a canopy of limbs overhead. There was a posted speed limit of twenty-five miles per hour and, because the state didn't believe in street lamps, often only headlights illuminated our way.

There were no sirens, just the lights slicing the still, deep night. We crawled by the scene, rubbernecking, and I saw a car had gone off the road and plunged into the woods. It was embedded among the trees at a strange angle, but it was intact and not crushed. My immediate sense was that the mishap wasn't fatal. When I was in flight school, we studied crash scenarios, so I knew the two things you needed to make it through were survivable G forces and survivable living space. The living space was definitely there, and how fast could you go on this winding country road? There was a man standing so casually by the street that at first I mistook him for the driver waiting expectantly for a tow truck. Another hectically flashing vehicle arrived, this one an ambulance. All will be okay, I reassured myself. The absence of sirens that were the adrenaline-pumping soundtrack to life-threatening emergency lulled me into a false sense of optimism.

Yet as we crept by, the gentleman—who turned out to be an off-duty police officer—and I locked eyes. In that split second, I saw his haunted expression. He was having a hard time holding himself together.

That's odd, I thought as we continued past. That accident didn't look so bad, but there was shock on that man's face.

"I saw a bloody hand," Ellie said.

The next day a blurb in the paper indicated nothing more than a South Kingstown youth had been in a one-car accident.

I went to a university basketball game that night with my friend Pat and her husband and we sat in the top tier of the arena, making a mess of the bag of popcorn between us.

"It's so awful about Zach," Pat remarked. "That kid who was in the car accident last night. He's on life support." Her daughter Ashley was classmates with him and along with others had kept vigil at the hospital for five hours that day. "She's awfully invested in this," Pat commented.

Details of the night before flooded back. The flashing blue lights, the innocuous looking automobile, that awful stare from the police officer. Ellie came home from school the next day with this news: Zach had died. "The principal announced it to us first period," she said. "Everyone was really quiet after that."

Rumors flew around our small town—that Zach had been driving too fast, that he'd ignored the stop sign, and that he'd been drinking. He wasn't wearing a seatbelt, which explained why the car was intact but his injuries were so severe. The family kept him on life support for a day while they said goodbye.

Ellie and I got in the car and returned to the meandering route we'd driven in the carefree hours after her Sweet Sixteen party. The turn in the road where the wrecked car had been was awash with newly placed crosses, flowers, gifts, and notes. Teenagers clustered around, clinging to one another and weeping openly. Two squad cars parked at either end of the somber queue—blue lights twittering—alerted oncoming traffic to the obstruction, while the other officers gestured for passing motorists to slow. It was a congested, pedestrian-clogged situation with at least a dozen cars parked on the shoulder and more arriving. Yet for the rest of the day and the next, law enforcement officials just maintained a respectful oversight on the impromptu memorial. How sensitive and kind of them, I thought, to let the kids grieve and ritualize it in their own way.

The principal brought all the district mental health counselors on board and even imported a few from South Shore. A service was held at the high school the following Saturday. But mostly the administration gave the students space and time to deal with the death.

After the funeral, I sat on my back deck in a fog of gloom, the bad news of the past several weeks settling on me like a noxious cloud. The week before, a fatal car accident involving a university student shared the headlines with the story of a teen from a different high school who "died of a gunshot wound to the head," a euphemism for suicide. And of course there was the Nelson girl, my former student and his two friends, and now Zach—a total of seven young, bright, beautiful lives snuffed out. They were all children belonging to this small community, and we were reeling.

I said to Ellie, "Always wear a seatbelt. Drive the speed limit. Obey the traffic signs. Don't get in a car with someone who's been drinking. Don't take chances when you drive." She exhaled dramatically. "Don't lecture me." Oh, someday you'll understand, my hazel-eyed beauty. Someday, when you're raw and eviscerated and smacked around by fate's fickle hand, you'll understand.

There was yet one more tragedy. Mom wrote me with the news that my uncle was diagnosed with an aggressive form of brain cancer and wasn't expected to live much longer. After he was given the diagnosis, he called my younger sister, a family physician, who told him with this particular cancer, he could expect to live twelve months at the most. "I'm going to do a lot better than that," he'd replied.

Several other relatives were in New York City visiting him, and my mom prevailed on us to take the train down for the day. Ellie, Joe, and I stood on the platform at the tiny Victorian station, gazing northward up the rails as if willing the engine to appear.

"I feel like I'm in a black-and-white movie," I commented.

"Of all the gin joints in the world," Ellie muttered.

"Exactly," I said, laughing. Some comic relief was needed for this journey.

When we arrived at my uncle's Brooklyn apartment, Jackie, his wife, put out her hand for Ellie. "Jackie," she said, introducing herself in a formal fashion. They shook solemnly. Then I walked over to Uncle David, who was sitting on the couch, and hugged him. "You remember my wee ones," I said, "Ellie and Joe." Thinking a handshake was the standard greeting in that household, Ellie again held out her hand, but David opened both arms. "Come here," he said, wrapping her in a big hug.

He looked cadaverous. His eyes were etched with deep, dark pockets, his skin pasty gray, and his hair was now completely white. In my mind, he was forever immortalized as the youthful uncle—the youngest by far of my mother's four siblings—who with his legendary intelligence and law degree had lit out for the big city and a dazzling legal career. The shell of a man before me bore no resemblance. He was impenetrable today, unable even to answer a simple question about the customary tip for a cab driver. David shuffled about, dragging his left foot along behind him, prompting my other uncle to observe that the fight had been knocked out of him.

His life had become a strict regimen of pharmaceuticals, radiation, chemotherapy, and medical appointments. In the kitchen there was a gallon plastic bag of medicine with an annotated spreadsheet of prescribed dosages and times. When he wasn't making trips to the oncologist in Manhattan, he watched television. Jackie assured me, however, that the presence of his family gave him a lift that lasted several days.

Always a first-rate cook and efficient, if impersonal, hostess, Jackie had prepared a pork roast with fresh green beans and an apple pie for dessert. It was a sunny fall day and we ate outside on the deck overlooking the Manhattan skyline. I remembered how many times I'd seen them through the years, either while we were living at West Point or in Northern Virginia or Rhode Island. I could explain the recent remodeling of their apartment to my other uncle and even noticed that the front foyer of the building had been retiled and repainted.

Several months later, I drove three hours back to the city, this time to a palliative care hospital—a hospice—in the Bronx. Impeccably dressed in pressed khakis and cashmere cardigan, full makeup, brunette hair smoothly styled—you'd never catch her in lavender velour loungers—Jackie spent her days in this room with her dying husband. Her laptop near the window enabled her to keep up with work e-mails.

"How late did you get home last night?" I asked. The women in my family were afraid she was on the brink of collapse. Still, she soldiered on, unwilling to accept assistance.

One of the reasons I came was because my mother and her sisters felt excluded from the care. Several months earlier, they and the other brother had formulated a plan to alternate coming to be David's at-home caregiver while Jackie worked. But she had brushed off their offer with a terse letter: "No visits longer than four days and never on the weekends." Her declaration left them all wondering what fleabag motel in New York City they could afford after buying a $500 plane ticket from Denver or Dallas. Ultimately, Jackie hired her cleaning lady to stay with David five days a week.

"This has all been very frustrating," my aunt in Colorado confessed.

"It's been a long goodbye, hasn't it?" And I meant since the day he married Jackie.

For years, we hadn't known how to respond to this intense, uptight control freak in four-inch pumps who isolated my uncle and then built the Maginot Line around him. Jackie was a rabid boundary setter who insisted David join her, which he usually did without argument.

Despite Jackie's palpable hostility and David's limp indifference, Brad and I, being the only family members on the East Coast, had managed to maintain a tenuous relationship with them over the years. David, the kid brother of my mother, had a special place in my heart. To my four sisters and me when we were growing up, he was the cool bachelor uncle who thrilled us with his visits. After my parents divorced, he became something of a surrogate father, although I sensed later that he never wanted the role and didn't like it, but that's how we felt about him.

I traveled down to the Bronx to report on things to my mother and aunts, but also to show Jackie that we loved her and we were there for her, because that's what family did. I brought a tin of whole leaf tea bags for her and, figuring she must be sick of the rubber chicken at the hospital cafeteria, sandwiches from my local gourmet shop—turkey and Swiss with mixed greens and champagne mustard. I also packed a book of poems by my friend Lisa Starr, the poet laureate of Rhode Island. Uncle David was an English major at Stanford and had earned the nickname Longfellow for his habit of reading and quoting poetry.

But he didn't want to hear the poems. He slept most of the time. Jackie and I made awkward small talk about my sisters and my children. I wondered how David got nutrition if he didn't eat. "All his systems are shutting down," she said. "He doesn't need much." I noted how frequently she tended to him—dabbing his chin, adjusting his pillow, smoothing his hair—a loving presence and solicitousness that none of the other terminal patients on the floor enjoyed. She said she called the nurses' station every night before she went to bed to make sure he wasn't in distress.

Jackie had always introduced me to acquaintances as "David's niece," a tic I found so grating that I wanted to say, "You married the guy. I'm your niece too." This time, she presented me to the rounding physician as "our niece" and the same way to the hospital chaplain later. Our niece. It was a small inroad.

The dreaded phone call came from my mother a few days later while I finished dinner. "David died this morning," she said. "I'll be in touch about funeral arrangements."

I lay my head on the dining room table, unable to stop crying. After all these months, after watching him fail before my eyes, after visiting him in hospice, I didn't expect it to hurt so much. Joe put both arms around me.

"It'll be alright, Mom."

Jackie's communiqué, written with blue fountain pen on twenty-pound cotton paper in her exquisite penmanship, provided point-by-point instructions for in-laws attending the funeral. My mother was allowed to read scripture at the mass; my other uncle to recite a poem graveside. She ended with an enjoinder to give David a "dignified send-off from this earth."

It crossed my mind, as I noted the stricken expression on Jackie's face when she walked behind the casket, that her life lesson from all this could be that there were some things we just can't control. I wondered if she got it.

She had marshaled the finest care, resources, specialists, treatments, therapy, and medications available. Privately, my mother and aunts believed that the cocktail of pharmaceuticals hampered David's ability to stay strong. We all agreed his quality of life in those final months was ruined.

Brad had sent me an article about a high-powered CEO who was diagnosed with terminal cancer. Rather than submit to an aggressive protocol, he chose no treatment at all. He compiled a list of people to whom he wanted say goodbye, then he and his wife reached out to folks as diverse as his fourth-grade teacher. Many closed their conversation with, "I won't say goodbye now because I'm sure I'll see you again." "No," he'd insisted, "this is it. Whatever we have to say to each other, say it now."

Such a different way to die, I mused—settling all your accounts with poignancy and meaning, rather than running out the clock taking pills to address the side effects from the last round of drugs.

I wondered how I would react if my end of life was no longer over yonder somewhere but knocking at my door. Would I go ahead and live balls to the walls for whatever time was left? Or, considering my two young children, would I grasp at any treatment for a chance, however slight, of extending my life and staying with them a few more months, and possibly, miraculously, being cured?

"Fight it with everything you've got," people were fond of saying. "You're in the battle of your life." How I hated the vocabulary of combat associated with cancer. There must be an alternative to struggling with the disease because that paradigm made your own body into a battleground. And have you ever seen a field post-battle? It's a churned-up wasteland littered with blood, body parts, bomb craters, and broken equipment.

What's another way to look at it?

"Surrender," my cousin said after the funeral. Waving that white flag was an act so inimical to our revolutionary-frontier-superpower American spirit that even speaking the words evoked a shudder. I surrender. I'm out of bullets. I'm out of ideas. I'm out of the driver's seat. I transfer the controls.

This approach smacked of hopelessness. A few days later, this insight came to me: Reclaim your life.

Confront whomever or whatever has stolen your life force and courageously take it back. Give attention only to the purposes and activities and relationships that reinforce your best self. We would all be served to ask ourselves regularly, "What would I do if I only had six months to live?" and then, by God, be about our business.

After the funeral, it was winter break in the school system, a time when our townsfolk traditionally bolted to the ski slopes in New Hampshire, Vermont, and Maine. I had considered taking the kids skiing for a few days, but after David's death I was too wiped out to organize anything or even to chauffeur short distances. I wasn't even sure I could get out of my pajamas. Ellie luxuriated in the unscheduled time, walking to the YMCA for workouts in the mornings, painting and crafting in her room or hanging out with friends at other times. Joe paced around the house like a caged animal and wore his fingers down to bloody stumps dialing to find anyone still in town. I felt bad for him and disappointed with myself that I couldn't step up, but I was so exhausted that I retreated to my bedroom.

Brad was deployed to Kosovo when 9/11 happened, out of the country when my grandmother died, gone now for yet another death in the family. With no understanding arms to collapse in, I faced these losses by myself and I was getting very tired. Shades drawn, I tunneled beneath the quilt on my bed, pulled the covers over my head, and slept.

8

NEW TRADITIONS, NEW NORMAL

Usually in December we hauled up our appliance-sized boxes of bows, garland, tablecloths, ornaments, and candles from the basement and decorated the house. This year, however, Brad's deployment to Afghanistan forced me to consider what yuletide traditions we'd actually observe. With a part-time job and the responsibilities of two parents on me, this holiday promised to be sparer than the past. Rather than wrestle years of trimmings up the stairs, I chose bits and pieces.

First off, because I knew it would be too depressing to rattle around our house alone during Christmas, Ellie, Joe, and I decided to fly to northern California to visit my sisters. They lived within a few minutes of each other and there was a joyful new addition—my four-month-old niece Kelly Ann.

In the meantime, I asked Ellie and Joe, "What do you need for it to feel like Christmas around here?" I wanted to establish our essential chords and then simply let the rest go. In the past, orchestrating all the sights and sounds of the season fell to me. This year had to be different.

While I assumed a tree was a given, they shrugged indifferently. I thought we might put up a small one early in December, but the idea of cutting a tree, hauling it home, installing it, lighting it, and decorating it just made me weary. That's a partner-assisted exercise. Instead I dropped by the Christmas tree farm, and the proprietor graciously loaded armfuls of pine and spruce cuttings into my minivan. I arranged them in the whiskey barrels and window boxes of my little house. I loved the classic look of evergreen and Christmas red.

And the annual Christmas letter? We military families are sentimental about that verbose narrative. It's our lifeline to each other, the spun gold that keeps us in touch over the years and continents. It pained me when I deleted that task, but because so many in our circle mentioned "Iraq" and "deployments" in their letters, I'm sure they understood. With a few mouse clicks, I ordered a photo Christmas card and called it done.

Presents were modest this year. Ellie declared she wanted no gifts, just contributions to her study abroad fund. I still bought her favorite tea and a calendar of vintage posters. Joe and I agreed the hefty ski club fee would be a large part of his holiday booty (but he would still find wool socks and ski gloves in his stocking). My sisters and I, collectively reaching diminishing scale of returns on materialism, agreed not to exchange.

There was a smattering of outings. Ellie and I strolled down to the local elementary school for the annual craft bazaar, that reassuring slice of Americana with its pipe cleaner snowflakes, themed basket raffles, and second graders singing "Rudolph the Red Nosed Reindeer." Joe went with me to the village Christmas tree lighting, where under a cloudless full moon sky, Santa Claus arrived by fire engine while the civic band played carols. (While we were gone, Ellie dyed her hair dark brown. But that's a story for another day.)

Starting on December 1, we hummed to the holiday CDs stacked next to the stereo and served dinner on stoneware sponge painted with snowy evergreens. No doubt we'd make a donation to the food drive and attend a Christmas Eve service. I would do a little baking—some sugar cookies perhaps—but certainly not the Herculean efforts of the past.

As for house decorations, I hung strands of icicle lights inside the windows on suction cup hooks I bought when Brad was assigned to Fort Campbell (translation: gone all the time) and I needed something I could put up by myself. I looped the lights around the hooks and plugged them in. This was my essential Christmas chord.

At the end of the day, I sat in the living room with a glass of dry red wine, turned off the lamps, and enjoyed the enchantment of tiny white lights glowing through sheer curtains. I felt steady, with just a little sadness and anxiety nibbling at the edges. I wasn't abuzz with that familiar holiday charge, but neither did I have the accompanying exhaustion, overwhelm, and unrealistic expectations I was so often saddled with in December.

Though Brad was overseas this year, we looked forward to his two-week leave in January, when we'd fill each day to the brim with activities. With that thought, I drained my wine glass, unplugged the white lights, and headed up to bed.

"When Dad comes home, I'm going to be right there with him wherever he goes."

This statement from Joe, who sat at the breakfast bar, made me stop what I was doing. While we had been rolling along without Brad and both kids seemed to be doing fine, these comments showed me how much they missed him.

By January, we were home from Christmas in California. Despite being back at school for the snowy New England slog, Ellie and Joe were giddy about Brad's mid-tour leave.

I wasn't so sure about it—his reentry into the household had always been disruptive. Our operations sans Dad were a well-oiled machine, and then suddenly he was back, brushing me aside and carrying on obliviously as if no time had passed.

This yearlong deployment to Afghanistan had revealed to me some unhealthy patterns in my marriage. When Brad was around, I was too close to the situation to have a useful perspective, but the longer we were apart, the more obvious they became. Significantly, over the years we had grown apart. For a long time there hadn't been much interpersonal communication between us, and what little there was existed on a functional level. I had tried unsuccessfully to gin up something more, but eventually lost heart because it was so one-sided. Despite my vow as a new wife to tend a lush relationship, we were one of those couples who talked approximately thirty-seven minutes a week, and that was mostly perfunctory logistical exchanges.

Where was the enthusiastic partnership I envisioned? What happened to that big, generous love I offered Brad in the beginning?

I thought he squandered it with inattention. He said I ruined it by complaining too much. We both agreed I'd withdrawn from him. We started conversations on this subject, but never finished them, choosing instead to put off the difficult dialogue for another day.

He stayed busy with demanding assignments and I took care of our children. His world enlarged while mine contracted to the four walls of our house. He trained in California and Jordan; I fluffed and folded laundry. He earned a Master's degree, a PhD, did research in London, and wrote a book. I ran the preschool carpool. He traveled to Germany, Korea, and the Balkans, while I reheated macaroni and cheese for dinner. I reminded myself over and over how valuable the work was that I did for our family, but a part of me struggled with this disparity in our fortunes. Didn't he remember when we were lieutenants together, both voraciously devouring the physical, mental, and intellectual challenges that came our way? Why would I be fulfilled having the neatest plastic wrap drawer on the block now?

A ration of grudges had surfaced since he'd left last June. What was I going to do?

I would do what I usually did: back off and give him a conquering hero moment with his adoring children. They would lavish attention on him, and he had two full weeks without distractions to soak it up. The needs of our young children had always provided ample diversion in our marriage, allowing us to focus on them and postpone the crucial couples conversations for later.

Brad's imminent return—if only for leave—meant it was time to bring the "Welcome Home" banner out of the basement and hang it. During Brad's first deployment to the Balkans in 2001, Ellie, Joe (who were both in elementary school), and I made a huge sign for him. I bought a six-by-nine-foot beige canvas drop cloth at the hardware store and sewed a casing on one end wide enough for a sturdy dowel. Then, using Ellie's artistry, we painted "Welcome Home Dad" in foot-high blue letters. Once it dried, we penciled in different sized stars onto the background and all of us, Joe too, took turns painting them red and gold. The effect was lovingly homespun yet dramatic.

On the day of his scheduled return from Kosovo (which, as any military spouse knew was always a moving target), the three of us hung the sign from the second-story window of our house. When we finished arranging it, the fifty-four square feet of greeting unfurled against red brick was a bold and satisfying sight. Because I knew Brad would arrive home in the middle of the night, I staked a floodlight in the front yard, angled up at our billboard so it shone like a welcoming beacon to a weary traveler.

After the brigade march on at the basketball courts, the happy and tearful reunion, the two kids chattering and clinging to their Dad like spastic birdies, we started home at three in the morning. Brad turned into our quiet neighborhood, illuminated only by the occasional porch light, and as we drove down the hill, he stared at the unexplained blob of light at the far end of our cul de sac. Once we closed in, his face lit up. There it was in all its glory: WELCOME HOME DAD! He couldn't stop chuckling, the way he did when he was happy beyond words, like when our babies were born. Ellie and Joe kept repeating "Do you like it Dad? We made it. Do you like it? Do you?" The next day I took a picture of the three of them in front of the house with the banner in the background. Brad had the biggest smile.

In years to come, our reunion sign got a lot of use. Sometimes we tacked it to the garage door or draped it on the tall bookshelves in the living room or casually in the front hallway if Brad had only been gone for a couple of weeks.

For Brad's mid-tour leave from Afghanistan, Ellie and I hung it from an upstairs window facing the street with Mr. Hippy shouting leveling instructions from the curb. Again, I focused a floodlight on it before we left for the airport to pick up Brad.

It was glowing in the dark when we returned (why was he always coming home in the middle of the night?), broadcasting our halfway milestone. We left it up for several days to announce his presence to the townsfolk, prompting a delivery of homemade chocolate chip cookies from my buddy Sue, spur of the moment visits from people passing by (including the owner of the auto parts store down the street), and enthusiastic telephone calls from neighbors.

One of my military spouse sisters with a similar sign shared a great idea to take it to the next level. Whenever she and her three boys traveled while her husband was gone, they brought the banner and a few thick-nibbed Sharpie pens of different colors. They asked friends and relatives to write personal messages on the back of the sign and date it. A couple of deployments (he had four) and numerous family trips later, she had a cherished family heirloom.

Years later, once Brad's military career came to an end, I boxed up our banner and shipped it to a young friend whose husband would soon be returning from his first deployment. I loved to think that after years of her use, she'll pass it on to another military family, where it will preside over more happy homecomings, soaking up the love and excitement.

The first day of Brad's leave was a red letter one for Ellie and Joe. They stayed home from school and hung out in their pajamas playing hooky. There were blueberry pancakes and bacon for breakfast, made with great fanfare by the three of them. I could hear the crashing and rattling of pans and nonstop chatter from my bed, where I was still reading. In a few moments, Brad stuck his head in the door to see if I needed a refill on my coffee. Of course I did. Bossy Mama, the one who kept the trains running on time, was temporarily out of service, and Mr. Good Time Guy was back. Or as I've said since Ellie was young: Mom is broccoli; Dad is cotton candy. The free-for-all had begun, and I planned to stay out of the way.

I overheard them talking about plans for the afternoon. Ellie's idea to go on a rugged rock climbing expedition won out and pretty soon, outfitted in polar fleece and hiking boots, they piled into the minivan and headed toward the hills of western Rhode Island. Quiet settled on the house and I knew Brad would take care of everything that day, including dinner, and I could stay in my pajamas. Maybe I would—the waters of fatigue that had been lapping for some time threatened to engulf me, like after finals in college when I straggled home and collapsed.

I was tired just watching Brad do the normal work of home and family. When he was gone, I stayed in survival mode, basically exhausted and sleep deprived for months but fueled by caffeine and necessity. When he came back, I had the luxury of realizing how tired I was and, better yet, sleeping it off. Three naps a day were common.

In contrast, Brad was fresh and energized after being sprung from his *Groundhog Day* existence in Kabul. He jogged on all the familiar town routes first thing in the morning, then got the kids ready and took them to school. In the afternoons, he happily accompanied Joe to the local town slope to see his newly acquired skills from ski club.

Brad also managed our weekends while he was home. He wanted to take us to the Performing Arts Center to see *Wicked* as a family, and he arranged everything—bought the tickets, made dinner reservations, and coordinated the linkup with Ellie, who had gone to her art class in the city. This was a lot of effort, I thought, even as I realized it was usually me doing it all. The receiving end was much more enjoyable.

The teacher of Ellie's global studies class invited Brad to give a talk, so he donned his uniform and obliged, bringing a burqa for the students to see and try on. They were amazed how tight and uncomfortable the headpiece was. He showed them lapis lazuli, garnet, and beads bought at the Afghan market. He brought out the map and described the mountainous terrain where he was assigned. In his slide show of pictures, the one of a goat in the back of a subcompact (an everyday scene there) was the class favorite.

Exemplary instructor that he was, he shaped this elaborate show and tell into a cohesive lesson to convey an understanding to high school sophomores about what was going on in that part of the world.

"Your Dad is so cool!" said one of Ellie's friends.

Having a deployed husband forced me to stay informed about national and world news because it was personal for me. Sunday morning found me camped in front of the television watching the talk shows digest the week's headlines. While I cooked dinner, I kept the television tuned to *PBS NewsHour* for in-depth discussion. I wanted to get a more balanced approach to news, something the liberal *Providence Journal* and the *New York Times* weren't giving me. "*Wall Street Journal*," my sister suggested. "TownHall.com," offered my mother. Right before he returned to Afghanistan, Brad fixed me up with the *Early Bird*, an aggregator that delivered news from many different sources and viewpoints to my inbox each morning.

There was a lot of upheaval going on just then. Sectarian violence in Iraq was escalating. In the states, Republicans lost control of both the House and the Senate in the mid-term elections. Pundits declared the outcome was a referendum on the war. Nancy Pelosi, the new Speaker of the House, said, "Bringing the war to an end is my highest priority as Speaker." At the same time, President Bush committed 20,000 additional troops (five Army brigades) in what became known as "the Surge" and replaced Secretary of Defense Rumsfeld with Robert Gates.

The Surge brought up the specter of extensions. Brad had floated this possibility before me ahead of time so I wouldn't be blindsided. "It could happen," he said. A twelve-month deployment could suddenly morph into eighteen months. We'd all heard the horror story of the brigade at the tail end of their deployment excitedly looking forward to going home, only to find out *on CNN* that they'd been extended an additional four months at the last minute. The chain of command later confirmed it. Badly handled! That's why I never made countdown chains for the kids, because return dates were an inexact science and we set ourselves up for disappointment if we fixated on one.

At least with the watershed of mid-tour leave, Ellie and Joe knew we were halfway through the year, and with Brad's help, I felt recharged enough to carry on through the turmoil and uncertainty. *Semper gumby*, I repeated. Always flexible.

The two-week leave drew to a close and soon it was once again the eve of departure with the same long faces, the same heart-to-hearts behind the same closed doors. As Brad and I drifted off to sleep, the parallel lines of our bodies occupied separate sides of the bed, and the barbed wire silence between us contained all that remained unsaid and unsolved. Not knowing where to start or what to do, we drifted further apart, pulled out to the deep by strong, unseen currents.

The airport scene the next morning was eerily similar to the one six months earlier—a long line at the skycap, our goodbye embrace at the curb, the stunned stares from onlookers, and my unexpected tears as Brad ducked into the terminal.

As quickly as he had come—like a meteor—he disappeared, and in stark contrast to his incandescent presence, the atmosphere at home became somber. Joe's obvious letdown at losing his Dad again tore me up. Ellie sat at the breakfast bar studying for mid-terms and complaining that she never took tests well. "I'm always the last one finished," she said. Her confidence slipped and my pep talks never held the sway her father's did.

I didn't anticipate the most draining part of deployment or leave—worrying about the effects on Ellie and Joe. As a mother, I obsessed about it, compensated for it, and tried to mitigate it with schedules and routines, but it remained there in my kitchen staring at me every day.

When customers swarmed the sports store for cleats, baseball pants, and tennis socks, and the Girl Scouts set up tables outside the supermarket selling cookies, it meant only one thing: spring had arrived.

In New England, Mother Nature doesn't let go of winter until April, and often not even then. On the first day of baseball practice there was still a chill. Spring pulled back the curtains a bit, teasing me with pale blue skies and a light breeze rustling through the still-bare trees. Joe, wearing last year's cleats that pinched and pants with patches at the knees, was up early, eager to get to the field. He even declined a sleepover the night before because he had practice at 9 a.m.

If there's an iconic harbinger of summer, it's skinny twelve-year-olds in baseball hats and jackets running laps around the baselines of a newly raked field. A friendly black lab with a red collar loped alongside them. Throwing and catching commenced, followed by turns in the batting cage. While raising Joe, I'd spent a lot of time at the ball park and came to appreciate this sport for the athleticism, Zen qualities, subtle intensity, and mental engagement it asked of its players. Also, who doesn't love a greasy cheeseburger from the snack bar?

The park thrummed with activity. At the nearby Easter egg hunt, echelons of little children lined up for their age-specific heats, and beyond that, high school girls competed in a soccer tournament. Parents on the perimeter watched from the comfort of their fold-up camp chairs.

Today was one of those chiffon-y mornings made all the more beloved by its fragility. Spring had been beautiful so far—forsythia had burst out in egg yolk yellow, Bradford pear trees bloomed like Austrian lace, and the tulip bulbs we buried in our front yard miraculously sprang forth.

Ellie and I planted pansies later that day. She held up a hunk of purple and white ones. "These are co-dominant pansies," she said, reciting lessons from sophomore biology. We dumped the dried pine boughs that had been in the window boxes since Christmas, and with Ellie's eye for arrangement, nestled the sweet little pansies in the dirt. They looked so cute with their leggy blossoms peeking out, shivering in the wind. "This is what the Easter bunny brought this year," I said, pointing to the flowers, "instead of candy to rot your teeth."

Angie, the twins' mom, had invited us to Easter dinner at their house, so the next day we strolled a few hundred yards down the bike path and navigated through a not-so-secret dirt trail into their backyard. This was village neighboring at its finest. I brought a covered dish of cheesy potatoes and an appetizer. Incomparable cook that she was, Angie made honey-baked ham, asparagus, parsnips, sweet potatoes, and dill biscuits. Together we mixed a designer drink for the occasion—the daffodil martini, or at least that's what we called it. Made with vodka,

Cointreau, and orange juice concentrate, it was more of a screwdriver, but it was a tasty toast.

Brad called to tell us he went to Easter mass at Our Lady of Providence, a place of worship run by the Italians in the coalition. "I gave the sign of peace to the four-star general in charge of the theater in Afghanistan," he said. After the mass finished, the priest asked everyone to stay in their seats. The Italian police had notified them there was a security issue and worshipers were to trickle out of the church in twos and threes rather than exiting all at once.

This was the season of reflection and I didn't feel like I'd done much preparation or purification this year. Unlike in the past, I didn't observe Lent or even attend Easter service. My spiritual life had atrophied this year, mainly because I didn't have a church or church family just then. The most I did was read my daily devotional and repeat positive intentions during yoga.

As welcome as spring was after the enforced cocooning of a long northeastern winter, it also increased our family operations tempo. Ellie had track practice and meets; Joe stayed busy with play rehearsals, baseball, and games. More specifically, it meant a lot more time behind the wheel for me. This was when I felt most acutely the absence of a second parent who could spell me in the driver's seat occasionally. I hustled home from the commissary to take Joe to his baseball pictures at the middle school, then shuttled him to his game at a park across town. Of course, that morning I had to do laundry because all his uniforms were dirty. After I dropped him at the dugout, I parked the car and sat in it for a while. I was hit with waves of exhaustion, compounded by PMS, pollen, and the recent time change. "I can't stay," I thought. This was one game I'd have to miss. Poor Joe. With his Dad gone I tried to be a parental presence at every game, both to support him and to report his progress to Brad, but I just couldn't do it that day. Another mother offered to take Joe home and I left. Bone tired, I dropped off to sleep on the couch, waking up just in time to pick Ellie up from track and deliver her to guitar lessons. Extracurriculars were strictly rationed to one sport per season per kid, plus music lessons. You wouldn't catch Ellie or Joe playing four club sports simultaneously like some of their friends did. Coordinating what little we did kept me busy enough.

Early one Saturday morning, after a last-minute trip to the grocery store to supply her with granola bars and drinks, I drove Ellie, or rather she drove because she had her learners' permit by then, to the school to catch the team bus to her track meet in Providence. "Did you drive?" squealed her friends, descending on her when she opened the door. As we hung out in the parking lot waiting for the others, I realized it was pretty cold and Ellie didn't have her warm-up jacket and pants. I drove home to get them. Back and forth, back and forth—that was my game this season.

Joe had to secure a ride to his own baseball game that day because I was headed to Ellie's meet later. Because I'd been to a lot of his games, he understood. I've tried to help the children realize that they do these sports because it's their thing, not because I'm providing constant reinforcement. Their motivation had to come internally, so even if I wasn't there, love of the sport kept them going. That said, I definitely tried to be a regular face in the stands cheering them on. The thing about deployment was that I could only do so much. For Joe especially, it was emotional when I wasn't there because his father was never among the group of dads at the games either. I often had to remind myself of something I heard an irate mother rant about once: "Don't tell me that I have to be at every ball game or I am not a good mother because, my friend, you are wrong!" When I couldn't go, I always spent a few moments with Ellie or Joe afterward to hear their post-game or post-meet report.

I'd given up both my part-time jobs by then because the psychological strain of working on top of single parenting was too much. I was paddling like hell underneath, but accomplishing so little. Trivial stuff filled my days, such as sending faxes, returning paperwork to the town hall, calling the refrigerator repairman, picking up branches from the storm, planting grass seed, cleaning the lawn furniture, getting the mower serviced, and exchanging our new dining room table for one that wasn't falling apart. This homemaker life amounted to eating soup in the rain at an outdoor café.

"It's just spring cleaning," a friend reminded me—not fulfilling but it must be done.

I tried to talk to Brad about the frustration of having too much to do and so many distractions and precious little contribution from either kid, who to be fair were busy with their own activities and school. My week, I complained, was full of logistics and driving with no time for personally satisfying pursuits such as writing.

"I spend my waking hours doing the shit work around here," I said.

"Yeah, the last couple weeks of deployment are the hardest," Brad responded. Once again I was rendered speechless by one of his comments.

"Listen to what I'm saying. Don't give me platitudes," I fumed. With my last nerve frayed, it didn't take much to set me off. This lead to an unfortunate showdown on the phone.

"Help me out here, Marna," he said. "I'm trying to be empathetic."

"You're trying to explain things away," I said. "I'm talking real life here and you give me meaningless crap."

Our phone call ended on a bad note, and for the rest of the day I felt remorseful that we wasted our few precious moments of conversation on an argument. I later received great advice from another military wife, who told me I should have coached my husband on what to say when I'm overwrought like that. Brad naturally went into problem-solving mode, but all I really needed him to say was, "It sounds really difficult. I wish I could be there to help. It won't be much longer. Hang in there." And if he said it like he really meant it, so much the better.

That night I picked Ellie up from a party at 11 p.m. and then fell right into bed. Then we were up at 6 a.m. to get ready to leave for an orientation session for foreign exchange students two hours away. When I said I needed to finish breakfast and put on my makeup, Ellie looked at the clock and pouted "We're going to be late!" Tired as I was from the late night pickup, her comment rubbed me the wrong way.

"Shut up," I yelled. "Just shut up." I was sick of her and Joe's sense of entitlement and their lack of appreciation for all I did. I stomped upstairs and slammed the door and finished getting ready. Ellie gave me the silent treatment for the rest of the day. Joe also froze me out when I refused his request to go to the movies (where middle schoolers converged on Fridays), a little event that cost me money, shot my evening, and required that I drive there and back—twice. I needed to have a little talk with both of them about all my responsibilities and how they should quit acting like brats.

Before I did it, Brad must have spoken with them because the following weekend, instead of pursuing their vigorous social lives, they both stayed home. Without complaints or attitude, Joe washed and vacuumed the car and Ellie gave the kitchen a deep cleaning and took my bike to the repair shop. We all raked the yard together. Then over a nice dinner that we cooked as a family, I apologized for my outbursts, and they assured me they would be more helpful in the future.

The storm passed and the clouds parted, ushering in sweet moments like Ellie riding up in the sunshine on her bike, blonde hair flying in the wind. Wearing a cornflower blue linen day dress she had foraged from my aunt's castoffs, she made such an enchanting sight that I impulsively greeted her with, "Hello Sunshine!" as she wheeled into our driveway.

"I feel like I should be carrying a fresh apple pie," she said breathlessly.

A few days later, Joe, without any context or leadup, said, "By the way, we're going out."

"Who?" I said, puzzled.

"Allie and me," he said. Oh, this was a big announcement. "Going out" was the middle school declaration to the world that they were a couple. Recent events made more sense now. When I dropped him off at the school dance, the twins and a third friend were in the car behind us, and I wondered why we hadn't carpooled. Apparently showing up with the guys wasn't done if you had arranged to meet your date at the dance. There was a protocol. My fellow mom spies reported Joe and Allie danced all three slow dances together. Joe had a girlfriend now and I was honored he confided in me because with Ellie I found out about everything through the grapevine.

While Joe was at baseball practice the following Saturday, Ellie and I took the tandem kayak to a local pond and paddled peacefully through the water lilies carpeting the pond's surface. It was so refreshing to be away from all demands and stimulation. Ellie inhaled the earthy scent of rhododendrons, reminiscing, "It smells like Rockbrook," meaning the camp she attended for several summers in North Carolina. After our short outdoor interlude, we strapped the long kayak onto a rolling cart to transport it back to the car, joking that it was like walking a very large lizard. Nature had soothed our souls and worked its healing magic on our strained relationship.

Brad asked me to put together some farewell presents for the Afghan general and colonel with whom he worked at the military academy. "Gift giving is a big deal in this culture and I'd like to give gifts when I leave that are worthy of the relationships I've developed," he wrote. He requested two nice Rhode Island prints, matted and framed, which I found at an art gallery in Newport for more than he probably wanted to spend. Both beautifully wrought watercolor reproductions were created with the giclee technique that made them nearly indistinguishable from originals; one was of a Rhode Island lighthouse and the other was of the Newport Bridge. On each frame, he wanted a brass plate engraved with a personalized message. For those, I went to a store called Signatures and placed a custom order. "They'll be done Wednesday," said the sales associate.

In the meantime, I collected the rest of the booty Brad wanted. At the Naval War College gift shop I purchased eight small presents for him to distribute to his nearest and dearest, including some money clips and a handful of War College challenge coins (the military equivalent of Pokémon cards). Then I went to the Navy Exchange and bought make-up for the Afghan officers' wives because only inferior products were available to them in Kabul. I filled two cosmetics bags with all manner of blushes, foundation, eyeshadow, liner, lipstick, powder, and brushes.

I drove back to Newport two days later and the brass plates were done except for one thing: they were inexplicably discolored. The own-er couldn't figure out why but offered to redo them right away. I said I'd pick them up after I rushed to the commissary for a few things ("few" being one of the big lies we tell ourselves). Too pressed for time after grocery shopping, however, I couldn't return for the plates that day because I had to rush home to take Joe to play practice. That meant a return trip to Newport the next day, my third in a week.

The following morning, I stopped by the florist's dumpster where I customarily scrounged for boxes, found a perfect-sized one, took it home, and consolidated all the miscellaneous packing material I could find. I carefully wrapped the framed prints in bubble wrap and nestled coins and money clips in a smaller box with crumpled tissue paper. I stuck some colorful gift bags and more tissue paper in with the makeup kits to make a better presentation later, hoping against hope they would make the long journey intact. Any dead spaces in the box were then filled with paper or bubble wrap.

I completed the customs form, which I could practically do with my eyes closed, addressed the box but left it open, then loaded the entire production in the car for the final trip back to Signatures to pick up the brass plates. By then the owner, a Vietnam era military wife, was my new best friend, called me sister, bought my book, and asked me to autograph it.

The new brass plates were wrapped and tucked inside, then I shut the box using copious amounts of tape, especially on the corners because I noticed packages to and from Afghanistan got really beaten up.

The box was quite large, a fact that made the postal clerk wince as I heaved it onto the counter. I watched anxiously as she measured and remeasured, checking the dimensions against her charts.

"What are those 'coins' on the customs form?" she asked. "That might be a problem."

"They're not legal tender," I assured her. "They're just trading coins."

"You better make that clear." I scratched in "collectible trading" next to "coins."

Then with a sigh, a wink, and a nod, she blessed the oversized package and sent it through. I bought enough insurance to cover all the merchandise inside plus some, grateful to finish a task that had taken me the better part of the week. It was important to Brad and I wanted to help. I'm sure he had no idea how much work his simple request generated!

"Everything is in there and if you don't get it within two weeks, let me know," I e-mailed him. "Go through the whole box because there are several subpackages."

Seven days later, he reported that he'd received the package and was thrilled with the contents. "Of course you did a far better job than I could have," he said.

He later told me a funny postscript to the parting gifts episode. At the group farewell, when he presented the painting to the general, he compared his colleague to the lighthouse depicted there—a beacon and guide to others. The Afghan stopped translating and whispered to Brad in English, "Sir, Afghanistan is a landlocked country. We don't have lighthouses here. They won't know what it means." Brad quickly backtracked to explain why lighthouses were important in our coastal state and so iconic to our country.

Brad has been shipping boxes home—boxes filled with the sport coats he had custom made in Afghanistan, boots and uniforms, belongings he didn't have space for or didn't want to carry home. This created a tiny dilemma: Where was I going to put them? His closet now contained my off-season wool pants, skirts, blazers, and dark sweaters. I had spread into all the empty space and, frankly, liked it that way. "Don't worry, hon. I'll fix up a rack for you in the garage," I joked.

"Get your stuff out of my closet!" he scolded.

There was a more disturbing subtext though. I didn't know how Brad was going to fit back into this marriage. I was happier and more peaceful without him. While Brad's e-mails and letters were full of rosy anticipation about homecoming, it meant a return to his habit of marginalizing and dismissing me after I'd been independent for a year. I'd had lots of time to think about things and there was no way I could tolerate that behavior anymore.

At my twenty-fifth high school reunion, I'd brought a photograph in case anyone asked about my husband. "He's in Afghanistan," I said, pulling the 5 x 7 out of its envelope. Taken at the last formal we'd attended, it was the classic portrait of a military couple—me in a red taffeta full-length gown, beautician-styled hair, and bling-y shoulder duster earrings. He wore his spiffy blues, and the awards on his chest were set off nicely by the deep color of my gown.

"He makes us all look like pussies," said one of my classmates. Another, a firefighter, asked for Brad's address in Afghanistan and actually wrote him a letter later, although they'd never even met. But it was this question, asked by my girlfriend during one of those late night, half-drunk confessionals, that took me by surprise.

"How do you stay in love when you're always apart?"

Yes, that was the emotional dilemma at the heart of it all. How do you stay in love? It was the wolf howling at the back door. Of course we grew apart. Time, distance, and the natural law of entropy had left a swath of destruction and no one in this situation escaped unscathed. The demands of transitioning into and out of couplehood were formidable, and with Brad's frequent absences, they had battered us for years.

When the times apart stacked and layered upon one another without a full reset in between, I became a petulant toddler, like our neighbor's son who refused to hug his father, look at him, or even go near him when he came home after a trip. All his parents could do was wait until the boy came around, which he did in his own good time—easing quietly up to his dad, deigning to spend a moment with him, perhaps a touch. Sometimes it took a day or two, sometimes more, depending on the length of the absence, but he came around eventually. Grappling with my own conflicting emotions, I felt similar ambivalence toward Brad as I tiptoed from room to room avoiding him. This felt like a minefield, not a marriage. "How do you stay in love?" my friend wanted to know. I wasn't sure we had.

There was also this: A marriage left alone quickly became feral.

Delusions and coping mechanisms disintegrated. All the issues and hurts swept under the rug over the years formed an uprising. The seemingly harmless garter snakes that slithered under the front porch emerged during deployment as a fifteen-foot mutated anaconda. It was hungry. And mad.

Our standard conflict avoidance, as it turned out, was only a stopgap measure. Hitting the snooze button all the time had seemed like an easy solution, but the problems we ignored didn't vanish. They just waited patiently and started a rave while Brad was gone.

My consciousness repopulated with unresolved burdens, plutonium grudges, and concessions I made that never sat well. Enforced separations peeled off the veneer of our relationship, revealing the worm-eaten surfaces underneath. I've seen even short intervals apart do a whopper on a marriage. An acquaintance and her four-year-old son bunked with her parents while a plumbing backup was fixed at their house. It took less than a week away from her husband for her considerable discontent to unmask. By the fifth day, instead of moving back home with him, she filed for divorce.

Once while deployed to Central America as a lieutenant, I watched an off-duty warrant officer drink himself silly, after which he read aloud a letter from his wife. Both in their early twenties, they had only been married a short time. He slurred and squinted as he tried to make out the words that had prompted his bender: "I've gotten used to doing things a certain way while you're gone," she wrote. "I like being independent. Things will be different when you get back." They had only been apart four months. He balled up the letter and staggered to his bunk, babbling "thish ridiculish booolssshit."

The relationship he left wasn't the one waiting for him. When he returned to his high school sweetheart, he was in for a rocky reunion that would either destroy his new marriage or present new and unexpected paths forward.

That's how I felt as I walked the perimeter of my marriage and surveyed, in the relentless high noon glare, our baggage with its years of waxy buildup.

Anyone who has moved with the military knows what it feels like to see your worldly goods stacked up on the sidewalk. Removed from their pleasing arrangements that imparted a sense of rootedness, they looked adrift and destitute, every scratch and dent accentuated. The spaghetti sauce stain on the area rug really popped—I'd long ago trained myself to overlook it. Those lamps we bought at a yard sale were unbearably tacky. My couch was dated and faded. The new perspective was brutal.

During Brad's absence, I identified feelings I hadn't been strong enough to confront before. Long-dormant issues and discord that were never completely explored or released reasserted themselves. When Brad came home, we'd have to ask and answer the all-important question: "Can we reinvent our relationship, not just return it to the way it was?"

Perhaps something more authentic and agreeable to both of us would evolve under this scrutiny, but I wasn't sure we could survive the transition.

Do you stay in love when you're always apart? We would soon find out.

As Joe and I hurried into the airport to meet Brad after his year in Afghanistan, I considered how different this was compared to his brigade's return from Kosovo.

We lived far from Army posts like Forts Bragg, Hood, and Campbell and their familiar fanfare. We didn't tape handmade signs to the gymnasium walls, cheer wildly when the battalions marched on, or share the giddiness with friends and family.

This time, Brad returned by himself to a civilian airport.

His sendoff ceremony a year earlier took place on the curb next to the skycap, minivan idling alongside us. Our two children still slept soundly in their beds at that early morning hour. Because Brad didn't even want me to accompany him into the airport, he said goodbye, hoisted the duffel bag on his sturdy shoulders, and disappeared into the terminal without a backwards glance.

Twelve months later, his welcoming committee wasn't even full strength. Ellie was attending her state sports banquet, so only Joe and I lingered awkwardly by the ticket counters, eyeing the cordoned chute where passengers emerged from the secure area.

Though it was nearly 10 p.m., the terminal buzzed with summer travelers.

"There he is!" Joe shouted, launching himself toward the tall, tanned figure in uniform striding toward us. He slammed into Brad's waiting arms at full force and they clung to each other like castaways after a rescue. Then it was my turn for a long, crushing embrace. The three of us hugged and laughed and sobbed, overwhelmed by the emotion of a demanding year and his safe return.

When we finally pulled ourselves apart from our very public display, I noticed a cluster of people staring at us. One woman stepped forward and, pointing at my camera, shyly asked, "May I take a picture for you?" She had tears in her eyes, as did the others, who by this time had formed a kindly circle around us.

An older gentleman reached out his arm. "Thank you for your service to our country," he said, shaking Brad's hand vigorously.

Brad steered us to the escalator, tired after his flight around the world and eager to get home. "God bless you and your family," a woman called out after us. I waved and smiled at her.

As we descended to the baggage claim, Brad told me that when the flight attendant announced his arrival home, the entire planeload of people applauded and let him disembark first.

Joe searched for the olive drab duffel bag while Brad enjoyed the rock star status of locals back slapping him and welcoming him home. I felt a gentle touch on my shoulder and turned to see a vacationer in shorts and T-shirt.

"Good to have him back, I bet," said the man. "We appreciate what you did too." Only when he walked away did I notice the "USMC" tattooed on his ankle.

It was a surprising reunion. I feared a letdown because we didn't have the bands, the pomp, and the kindred crowd of our Army community. Instead the local citizenry blessed us with their spontaneous and genuine outpouring of patriotism and compassion.

9

FITTING BACK TOGETHER

The local Little League wanted Brad to throw out the first pitch at Joe's game when he got home.

"Should we just surprise him?" the league commissioner wanted to know.

"Let's tell him ahead of time," I said. "He'll want to practice his pitch so he doesn't throw a worm killer."

At the opening game, the coaches from the lower field brought their boys up to be a part of the ceremony, and they took their spots on the baseline with the other two teams. The national anthem began, and each player placed his hat on his heart.

Then the announcer introduced Brad. I had previously given the commissioner a short summary of what Brad had done in Afghanistan the past year and in the Army for the past twenty-two years, starting with graduation from West Point and what he would do next.

Brad walked up to the pitcher's mound and donned his Little League baseball hat. Joe was the appointed catcher, and if there's a more endearing sight than a twelve-year-old in full catcher's gear and helmet squatting behind home plate punching his mitt, all intensity and focus, I've never seen it. In this case, the catcher was also beaming with pride. To me it was a perfect line segment with father at one end, son at the other. Brad wound up in his graceful, athletic way and sailed a fast ball over home plate, which snapped into Joe's glove with a satisfying report. Joe lifted his catcher's mask and jogged the ball back to the mound. Father and son exchanged a solemn handshake and nod—the classic baseball ritual. That was the moment captured by a photographer from the local paper, a snapshot that appeared in the sports section the following week. That was the picture I stuck to the refrigerator and taped next to Joe's bed and memorialized in our scrapbook and showed around at our next family reunion. Just to make this event even more memorable, Joe's team won.

A month after the deployment, we drove Ellie, who was leaving to spend her junior year of high school in Argentina, back to the same airport where Joe and I had just picked up Brad. She didn't get her first choice of Spain; there were problems with the packet we had so methodically assembled. The transcripts that we received from the high school in a secured envelope weren't certified with a raised seal. There wasn't a copy of her passport (it was still being processed) and the physical examination was missing a respiration rate. By the time we fixed everything, all the slots to Spain were filled. Ellie received the news in a phone call, turning away from me so I couldn't see her crying.

Her disappointment, as my children's always did, weighed on me. "Trust the processes of life," I consoled her. There were times in my life when things didn't unfold the way I wanted—the job I sought went to someone else, for example. It worked out because later I found another position for more pay. "Something better is on the horizon," I said.

Ellie accepted with equanimity the change in plans and set about preparing for Argentina, beginning with labeling every item in the house she could reach—*el azúcar* on the sugar bowl, *la plata* on the silverware drawer, *la medicina* on the basket of prescriptions. Each week she wrote three new words on the kitchen chalk board to memorize: "*el corazón* (the heart), *la cuchara* (the spoon), *el pollo* (the chicken)." In the evenings, I found her at the computer clicking through her Rosetta Stone language lessons and practicing pronunciations.

I pointed to a sign written in Spanish on the city bus we rode and asked her to translate it. "THE—something, something, OF, something, something, something"; she mumbled through the unfamiliar parts and spoke the articles and prepositions with great enthusiasm. It was right before she left, and I realized she was far from fluent. Oh well—Ellie couldn't be the only American student who went to a foreign country without knowing the language.

It would be the first of many times I accompanied Ellie to the airport and cried in the terminal as she strode off, backpack slung over one shoulder, to the departure gate and her next destination, eager for an adventure in a new country or a different part of the United States. We always joked that she made her first interstate move at four hours old when we drove from the birth center in Maryland to our home in Virginia. Since then, our military brat moved eight times, and though I worried about her, I realized she had developed a facility for engaging people and places with poise and self-confidence.

Ellie had stripped the posters and personal effects from her room and left it as tidy as a guest space, but her absence created a vacuum in the household. "Where's my dishwasher emptier?" Brad lamented. Once I found him in tears at the kitchen sink. "I was just thinking about Ellie and the spirit she brings to this house," he said. Something wasn't missing in the family; something new was present, a heavy, oppressive feeling. Was it grief?

"That's how we felt when our oldest left for college," a friend said.

Joe benefitted from the fallout. In our sadness and vulnerability, we spoiled our only son and he happily obliged us. A surfboard? A new bike? Snow skis? Certainly.

"It's easier to run the house and make decisions when the alpha dog isn't around," a friend said after her husband returned from Iraq. What happened when the alpha dog returned? A tortured transition, to say the least. "If he keeps up with the attitude, I'm gonna have to kick his ass," she fumed. This was a condition we referred to as "the fiery re-entry."

Despite romantic, rose-colored expectations, reunions were often amped-up versions of pushing each other's buttons. During three years of successive absences at Fort Campbell, Brad and I learned more coping skills than we ever thought necessary. Each time he came home, it felt like he was intruding. The first twenty-four to forty-eight hours—when he was oblivious and I was hair trigger impatient—were the worst. Sometimes he was only home for two days before he left again and we hadn't even stopped growling at each other yet. When that happened several times in a row, it felt like there'd been a sanitation strike and our garbage hadn't been picked up for weeks. It was just icky.

I was certain there would be a rocky reintegration period after a yearlong deployment, so I anticipated ways to ease the pain. Brad was content when his hours were filled with productive, autonomous work, preferably of the hands-on variety, so I compiled a honey-do list as long as his arm. My intention was to keep him occupied so we could sort things out at a reasonable pace. Plus, remembering his built-in allergy to home improvements, this was perhaps the only time he'd agree to tackle projects around the house.

At first glance, the honey-do list I began looked harmless enough, but a funny thing happened as I wrote—the fifteen-foot mutated anaconda thrashed around under the porch. Brad dubbed the note I posted on the refrigerator my "Reintegration Manifesto." At the top it said "Husband: Read and Obey." The opening paragraph proposed attitudes he should adopt as we began this transition. *No resistance. Joyful! Joyful! Agreeable. No Grumpiness. Cheerful. Questions are okay—Objections are not okay. Trust Marna's vision, TRUST her.*

And so it began:

1. Remove old pedestrian door on garage and install new one.
2. Take down fence section on north end of deck.
3. Hang new bulkhead door so it swings the other way.
4. Rebuild deck steps to Marna's specifications.
5. Plant another row of arborvitae.
6. Do not proceed in a vacuum, but clarify, notify, and remember: Marna is the subject matter expert (SME) on home and family.
7. Help put stuff together for yard sale.
8. Build Marna a potting bench next to garage.
9. Design hanging structure for Topsy Turvy tomato planters.

Such a flurry of activity commenced. While my batteries predictably dribbled out their last traces of power, Brad was literally whistling while he worked, merrily crossing off tasks at the rate of three men and adding new ones every day:

10. Install screen door.
11. Power wash and treat deck.
12. Build cucumber climber.
13. Buy new outdoor light fixtures.

That's how we passed the first few weeks of his return—in a fragile domestic peace, with him contentedly reengaging in the life of the home, eager to grocery shop, fix dinner, or run to the middle school and sign Joe's permission slip in the middle of the day. He wanted to look for a new truck and take us out to dinner and watch baseball games in the camp chairs and be hugged and welcomed home by our close community. It was all well and good.

We still had to face the deep misgivings I'd identified the previous year, the fifteen-foot mutated anaconda under the porch, and the inevitable distance between us. There was a public Reintegration Manifesto and a private one. The one I kept hidden was sure to be incendiary.

In July Brad dropped me off at the ferry to Martha's Vineyard, where I was headed for three days of rest and recreation (mainly rest) that I desperately needed after the demanding year. I took my bicycle and an overnighter of belongings, planning to alternate between riding around the island, reading, and sleeping. "I'll be home Thursday," I said. "I can't remember the time but it's around two. Do you want me to run inside and find out when the ferry arrives?"

"No, you wrote it down," he said. "I saw it on the kitchen counter."

"Okay. If anything changes, I'll call you," I said as we kissed goodbye and I rolled my bike up the ramp to the waiting boat.

When we moved to Rhode Island from an intense operational unit—the 101st Airborne Division—Brad's new ROTC command offered newcomers the benefit of six sessions with a marriage counselor to ease the transition back to semicivilian environs and a life of more togetherness. Many couples needed assistance detoxing and reconnecting after assignments during which important personal matters had been crowded out, and the military machine had ground them to bits. We accepted the help.

Our relationship counselor was a woman not much older than we were who had an office built on the side of her house, a rustic structure tucked in the woods. During our very first session she correctly deduced from my sullen silence that I was "in a cloud of resentment." She walked us through an exercise in which we had to compliment one another on two specific things and ended the hour by leading us in the affirmation, "I'm willing to let go and move forward with you."

After a few nondescript couple's sessions, Brad, citing work demands, quit attending and I continued going alone. Several more appointments followed with meandering dialogue that drew out my history but didn't seem to go anywhere. Finally the therapist suggested we try an energy technique similar to Reiki, which I was familiar with, so I agreed. I relaxed on a massage table in my clothes as she moved around me with her palms outstretched receiving impressions and attempting, as she explained, to "find and move stuck energy." Most of the time she was quiet and focused, except for this one question: "What happened when you were four? I'm getting a strong impression from that age."

I couldn't answer, but I asked my mother, and she prompted a vivid, visceral memory. I was sitting in the hot sun in the middle of a large asphalt parking lot, very uncomfortable, confused, and scared. My mother then filled in the back story. When I was four, she ran out of patience with my father and left, decamping with my three sisters and me to our grandmother's in Denver. My sisters were six, two, and one, and we thought it was just a fun vacation to grandma's for the summer. Somehow by the end of August, my father had persuaded mom to return, convincing her he'd turned over a new leaf, so we flew to Dulles, where my dad met us at the airport.

As we walked across the sun-stunned parking lot to our VW bus, I saw it was full of junk. At the beginning of the summer, we had moved from Oklahoma to Delaware in that vehicle, and it was still packed with the detritus of a family cross-country trip. Boxes, laundry baskets, bags, household goods, and fast food trash were piled on every square inch of seat, floor, and cargo space. I wondered, "Why didn't daddy clean this out? We've been gone a long time." My mother had the same thought at that moment because she launched into an epic screaming and swearing fit. Unlikely as it sounded, my dad hadn't thought to prepare the car for his family. Only the driver's seat was clear, but there was no place for any of us to sit during the hour drive back to the Air Force base.

We waited on the hot pavement, suitcases settled around us, as mom and dad yelled at each other. Then while my fuming parents churned through the contents of the vehicle, attempting to excavate room, we four frightened children were marched to an island of crab grass and plopped down beneath a parched sapling that afforded little protection from the August heat. No doubt my mother second-guessed the decision to return to her husband, and I wondered to this day why she didn't just corral us into the terminal and catch the next flight back to Denver.

When I brought this memory to the counselor, she asked me to write a letter to my dad about the incident and read it to her aloud. "It sounds like your dad had a problem with narcissism," she commented. "That would explain why you're hypersensitive to any signs of it in Brad or yourself."

My mantra, if unconscious and unarticulated most of my life, had been, "Don't be needy and don't be neurotic." In my marriage, I refrained from insisting on my needs because I didn't want to skate that ragged edge of self-absorption. It was the siren call of an abyss from which I would never return. My worry bordered on terror, like every moment of self-advocacy was only a gateway drug to full on narcissism.

This childhood memory represented a breakthrough for me, and I made the mistake of sharing it with Brad. He tucked it away for use later as a deflector whenever conflicts or accusations arose. "This isn't about me. It's about the four-year-old on the hot tarmac" was code for "It's your problem." The fact that he exhibited behavior similar to my father's, such as leaving me alone when I was in labor and refusing to come home when his daughter and wife were sick, was lost on him. Most of my problems with Brad through the years, I now realized, revolved around abandonment.

On Thursday afternoon, as scheduled, I returned from Martha's Vineyard to the dock that was situated on a remote, repurposed Navy base. During the especially rough ferry ride, I learned why the locals called it "the Vomit Comet" because I spent most of the journey clutching a sick bag and turning various shades of green. When I walked jelly-legged down the ramp to terra firma, Brad wasn't there. I checked both buildings. I walked up and down the aisles of the dirt parking lot looking for his car. I couldn't reach him on his cell phone, nor my daughter on hers. The other arriving passengers eventually disappeared, leaving me alone in a deserted area. Because I habitually ran late, I figured that's what happened to Brad, so I waited on the curb as the minutes ticked by, periodically calling his cell phone or the house landline. Inside the air-conditioned double-wide that served as a terminal, the television blared headline news at migraine-inducing volume, which kept me from waiting in there. Finally, I asked the ticket agent to call me a cab. "None available at the moment," she announced after checking. I dialed my cleaning lady. "Were Brad and the kids there this morning when you were at the house? Was everything okay?" "Yes," she answered. "Had anything happened?" No, not that she knew of.

And yet here I was sitting on the hot tarmac as the July sun beat down on me relentlessly. "Brad's not coming," I finally realized, and my temples throbbed like when something unbelievable has happened. The last phone number I dialed was to my neighbor, Rick, who kindly took time out of his workday to drive thirty minutes to the ferry stop and give me a lift in his electrician's van.

Brad had taken Joe fishing, as it turned out, to a pond with sketchy cell phone coverage. "You weren't at the ferry stop," I confronted him angrily when he returned.

"You said you'd call," he insisted.

I had written down the date and time of my return and confirmed it with him verbally. "I said if I decide to come home early, I'll call," I said.

This was the same miscommunication, misunderstanding, and lack of listening over and over again. I was furious that he forgot me. I was seething, trapped in an echo chamber of my own rage. This was about the four-year-old on the hot tarmac, yes, and it was also most assuredly about him and about us.

It was time—past time—to see another marriage counselor.

Our marriage was that ball of irredeemably tangled Christmas lights that I attempted to unsnarl every December before I got frustrated and carried it back to the attic.

The problems were too nuanced and sophisticated for us to treat ourselves. Conflict resolution was never our strong suit—we devolved quickly to defensiveness, counter accusations, strategic retreats, wall building, slow burns, and lingering resentments. Going for the jugular was our specialty, and we had very good aim.

It would take an objective therapist with the tools and patience we lacked to navigate these tricky conversations.

The one we chose was Dr. Brooks, a marriage counselor recommended by friends. A middle-aged man with a cozy office in town, Dr. Brooks was professorial looking in his cardigans and bow ties but personable and genuinely interested in helping us.

"I certainly sense the tension between you two," he commented during our first session.

Dr. Brooks was the fifth marriage counselor we'd seen over our seventeen-year marriage. He was also the first male one, a fact that may have contributed to what little progress we made with him.

After one productive session, Brad confessed, "You know, I always went to marriage counselors thinking you were the one with all the problems," he said. "For the first time I see we both have issues."

That explained why he usually dropped out of counseling, leaving me to continue alone. Brad was a rational man whose qualities made him a good Army officer but an obstinate husband. Throughout the marriage, I'd confronted the immutable trifecta of his hyperconventional upbringing, Catholic dogma, and cherished infantry swagger, such as, "If the Army wanted you to have a wife, they'd have issued you one."

I thought of marriage as a chance to love and be loved, to look after and nurture someone, to be his wingman and advocate. My naive belief was that Brad felt the same way, even after he failed to show up for me in big and small ways. I endured life's gauntlets without the unconditional love and protection of a husband, without the space where I was acknowledged, safe, cared for, heard, and noticed. The deployment only confirmed that I felt ignored and invisible in this union.

The marriage Brad left twelve months earlier was quietly crumbling. I was sad, frazzled, and lonely a good amount of the time, while he was moody and mute in response. We had been steadily, if not happily, wed for seventeen years and the relationship was less than bliss but better than disaster. At best, we peacefully coexisted with little emotional intimacy, but the worst spells were filled with banked bitterness.

Ours was a shaky attachment that never came together as planned, possibly because the tender years of bonding as a couple were crowded out by career demands, geographic separation, and parenting young children.

Early on we figured if we couldn't resolve contentious issues, we could ignore them and pretend. Getting along was a symptom of things going south due to us keeping our emotions bottled up. Admitting the gritty shortcomings and embarrassing frailties of our union took more courage, candor, and stamina that we could manage. We weren't in the habit of tending to our marriage. We had succumbed to the predators of fatigue and inattention.

When unstable weather patterns were predicted, meteorologists often warned that "conditions are right for a tornado." The marital twister had yet to materialize but the developing signs were all there—we just ignored the forecast.

It's as if we rolled the jalopy out of the garage and casually surveyed the back seat filled with yellowed newspapers, sun-faded Beanie Babies stuffed between the windshield and dash, litter-covered floor, hatchback secured with baling wire, muffler hanging by a thread, busted headlights, dry-rotted wiper blades, and expired license plates. Kicking the bald tires, we climbed in the passenger side door (the driver's side wouldn't open), settled ourselves on the ripped, rump-sprung upholstery, turned the ignition key, and when the heap sprang to life, said, "Let's take this baby on a long road trip."

Deployment didn't cause our problems; it unmasked them. Over the years, as we pushed things to the side, avoided scrutinizing, and averted our eyes, hairline cracks became craters.

Basic stuff got ignored when our partnership was on autopilot: Each other. Emotions. Empathy. Any knothole we didn't understand. If, when tremors occurred, we had stepped back and asked, "What's the message here? What reality isn't being acknowledged?" then every potential crisis could have been an opportunity for positive course correction, not a sinkhole that eventually swallowed us.

Often I ran across helpful articles with titles like "Make Your Marriage Deployment Ready," as if we could sit on the couch one evening and make it so in a single conversation over coffee. It wasn't something we could do in the weeks leading up to Brad's departure. A deployment-ready marriage must be a shared goal from the beginning, cultivated with openness, communication, respect, honesty, attention, and affection. It was an ongoing process requiring humility and a willingness to learn. That was a tall order for two fallible people who were busy dodging the slings and arrows of life.

Other couples did it, however, and successfully navigated the whitewater rapids of military life. That's why I don't blame the Army for our breakdown. We own it. Our disconnects, slights, and cruelties to each other through the years were responsible for the irreparable damage.

The marriage was troubled beforehand, but a year apart made it unsalvageable. Deployment was the death knell.

"I know I've done things that have hurt you deeply," Brad admitted in a letter to me during our counseling with Dr. Brooks, "And for that, I'm truly sorry."

There was movement in the right direction, but much had been overlooked in the intervening fifteen, sixteen, seventeen years. Accumulated misunderstandings had leached poison and toxins into our relationship. We built a marriage on unacknowledged early pain that had engraved its memory on my flesh. That was a long time for him to shrug when he knew I had been wounded at his hand and a long time for me to dwell in doubt about the core beliefs of my husband.

"Do you even have one foot in this marriage?" Dr. Brooks flat out asked me.

"Not a whole foot," I answered. "Maybe a toe."

And "maybe a toe" was overstating it. I had emotionally moved out and packed my belongings in the U-Haul, waiting for the final scene to finish.

"You knew what you were getting into."

Nothing, but nothing, annoyed me more than this insipid platitude. It was a stale, off-the-rack response to the complex and serious challenges facing military couples after fifteen years of war.

In regrettable point of fact, I didn't know what I was getting into. When we married, there was no Global War on Terror with multiple and sometimes back-to-back deployments to the Middle East. At the time, the six-month task forces to hot spots around the world had been reduced to four months because half a year was "too long to be away."

We didn't have kids when we got married. Obviously, never having children, I didn't realize motherhood would change my life so dramatically while Brad's as a father would continue apace. When children arrived, the contract had to be renegotiated because the terms were different. Marriage wasn't a snapshot preserved under glass from the moment of the vows. It was a living, growing entity that required monitoring and accommodation. Trauma, drama, and milestones created imbalances. Adjusting to them was the business of being human, of being yoked together during all our vulnerable, crazy, weak, temperamental moments. It asked more of us than tired clichés.

Second, can we ever really know anyone or anything beforehand? People are unpredictable and complicated. Situations are fluid. It was one thing to see some behavior and delude yourself into believing that "this will change." It's quite another to anticipate everything the future holds.

"You knew what you were getting into." Consider this banality applied to other contexts. If it were true, no one would ever leave a job or transfer from a university or sell a home that once seemed like the perfect fit. Business partnerships would never unravel or elected officials get voted out of office because all parties knew exactly what they were getting into.

There's knowing it and actually living it, and sometimes they're worlds apart. "You knew what you were getting into" was just a trite response to avoid engaging in difficult discourse.

A crucible is a severe searching test or trial, a place or situation that forces people to change. This year was our crucible. Our workaday routine held up when we were together but fell apart during deployment. The stress and separation forced long-simmering issues to a full boil, and we could no longer keep up our method of inattention.

There was also time to think and quietude to reflect on my discontent. While Brad was gone, I allowed myself to feel concerns that I had stuffed down for years.

"Stop agreeing to things that insult your soul and wake up!" an advice columnist admonished her readers. I had consented to an arrangement that cast me as an extra in Brad's traveling road show. Subverting my identity in service to his career and the well-being of our family was the path I easily slipped into. If I had worked outside the home all along, if we had more evenly shared the home keeping and child care responsibilities from the beginning, Brad might have seen me as an equal partner with my own goals, not someone content to be absorbed into his life. He scarcely noticed as I scraped my soul bare filling logistical roles while huge parts of me withered from neglect. We never had the critical conversations about what compromises it would take to repair this and if we were prepared for the sacrifices. Creative solutions needed to be implemented, but they weren't, and for that we're both to blame.

EPILOGUE

Less than a year after Brad's return from Afghanistan, we separated, and two years afterward our divorce was finalized. By then we had been married for over two decades, which took us through the nineties, Y2K, the dawn of the twenty-first century, 9/11, and the Global War on Terror.

The decision to end our marriage was heart-wrenching. With my wedding vows, I believed I would be part of an enduring union, and failing at that brought profound sadness. After living with my parents' divorce as a child, I didn't want to put my kids through the same ordeal. When even five marriage counselors couldn't help us mend the relationship, I did everything I could to mitigate the negative effects of the split on Ellie and Joe. They remained in the family home with me and continued at the same schools in the village that had become the de facto hometown for two military brats after five years. Brad moved to his own place nearby and saw them often.

Because it was a troubled marriage, being released from it was a relief for me, but for Brad the opposite was true. Having a full-time stay-at-home spouse had always enabled him to pursue his career and work he loved with the assurance that I would take care of everything in his absence. Unfortunately, this imbalanced arrangement created a lot of resentment between us. He enjoyed professional satisfaction but paid for it later with the painful dissolution of his marriage.

Did we give our marriage over to the military all those years ago? It's closer to say I gave myself over to a man who folded me into his ambition and never considered my unfulfilled wants and needs left in its wake.

There were many failures we could talk about on both sides: failure to connect, failure to speak up, failure to listen, failure to act. The biggest was a failure of imagination. We didn't look in the same direction and create the kind of partnership in which we could both thrive. Instead we relied on tropes, conventions, and shopworn stereotypes, and they failed us miserably.

Even strong relationships decay over time with the kinds of pressures military life and deployment bring. When we were separated for weeks, months, or years, there was less common ground and fewer shared moments. We grew apart. I was ready to make sacrifices for what I was passionate about—him, our children, service—but for so long this path had asked for too much, far more than I was prepared to give. There was ultimately heartache despite an attitude of perseverance. As a nation, we're only just beginning to assess the damages of this war, and no doubt service members, children, and marriages have borne the consequences of our long involvement.

ABOUT THE AUTHOR

Marna Ashburn grew up in an Air Force family, served five years in the US Army as a helicopter pilot after college, and was then a military wife for twenty years. Ashburn is the author of many books and articles on military life and military families, including *Household Baggage: The Moving Life of a Military Wife* (2006) and *Household Baggage Handlers: 56 Stories from the Hearts and Lives of Military Wives* (2008). She has been a featured guest speaker at Spouse Club meetings at military installations across the country, including Fort Leavenworth, Fort Drum, Fort Irwin, Fort Polk, the US Military Academy, Hanscom Air Force Base, Carlisle Barracks, and the Naval War College, and has been interviewed several times on Army Wife Talk Radio (AWTN.com) and SpouseBuzz.com. She was a regular monthly columnist for *Military Spouse* magazine, and her other articles and essays were featured in publications such as *Off Duty*, *Married to the Military*, *American Baby*, *Skirt!*, *The Military Times*, *SO Rhode Island*, and the *Providence Journal*. Her books can be found at her website, HouseholdBaggage.com, which also links to her blog, *The Chronicles of Marna*.